COMMUNITY LAW CENTRES

To Fred Walling
Sadly missed but whose
example remains an inspiration
to all those who knew
and loved him

Community Law Centres

A critical appraisal

MIKE STEPHENS
Lecturer in Social Administration
Loughborough University

Avebury

Aldershot · Brookfield USA · Hong Kong · Singapore · Sydney

Published by
Avebury
Gower Publishing Company Limited
Gower House
Croft Road
Aldershot
Hants GU11 3HR
England

Gower Publishing Company
Old Post Road
Brookfield
Vermont 05036
USA

ISBN 1 85628 083 7

Printed and Bound in Great Britain by
Athenaeum Press Ltd., Newcastle upon Tyne.

Contents

Preface

The law in England and Wales is not only a defence of the citizen against arbitrary power and injustice, it is also a means whereby individuals may assert their rights. Law centres are one of the more recent innovations in the legal sphere dedicated to ensuring greater access to law so that citizens may be better able to know their rights and to pursue them effectively. Community or neighbourhood law centres, many of which are located in inner – city areas, constitute the voluntary sector in the delivery of legal services. They receive funds from various charities, local and central government, and from the Legal Aid scheme. Moreover, their lawyers are salaried employees and, therefore, the centres do not operate like private solicitors who typically charge a fee for service. In addition, law centres are specialists in those areas of law, particularly civil law, which are of most relevance to poor and low – income individuals. It is these groups that comprise the majority of law centres' clientele. In common with many private solicitors, law centres conduct work on behalf of clients under the Legal Aid scheme, but unlike private solicitors law centre lawyers often work in partnership with other professionals, such as social and community workers who are also employees of law centres.

This book is concerned to explore and evaluate the work of British law centres and, in particular, to assess their contribution to the realization of citizenship rights. The concept of citizenship and the rights associated with it are discussed in the first chapter, along with a consideration of the ideas of public participation in decision – making processes and the worth of competent citizens able to pursue their rights effectively. In Chapter Two I cover the reactive and proactive manner in which the law may be mobilized to deliver legal services. The reactive and proactive delivery mechanisms have an important influence on the operational structure of law centres, which in turn may be described as either reactive, open – door centres, or proactive, closed – door centres. Open – door centres tend to individualize the problems clients bring to them, whereas in closed – door, proactive centres there is a greater focus on group and community work activities. These different delivery mechanisms also influence the nature of the lawyer – client relationship, which is another issue covered in Chapter Two.

In the following chapter I analyse the origins and formative development of law centres in the UK, and I explain how the majority of centres adopted a predominantly open – door and reactive approach. The major themes of Chapter Four are the operational difficulties encountered by reactive, open – door law centres, and the extent to which they contribute to the development of competent citizens. Drawing on the experiences of a number of such centres and on a detailed case – study of a typical reactive agency, I describe the range of operational problems they encounter, and analyse their contribution to the notion of active citizenship. In contrast to the reactive delivery of legal services is the proactive approach, which is the subject of Chapter Five. Here I outline the work and goals of proactive law centres. Again using a detailed case – study I assess the contribution that this operational philosophy can make to the realization of active and competent citizens. I should point out that in both case – studies, involving agencies that I have called the Urban Community Law Centre and the Northern Neighbourhood Law Centre, the names of these two centres (and of other groups and institutions in contact with them) have been fictionalized in order to preserve the anonymity of all those concerned.

The story of the law centre movement in the 1980s forms the focus of Chapter Six. I note the continuing difficulties facing law centres as well as commenting on the movement's innovative developments in meeting the needs of clients. Finally, in Chapter Seven, I discuss the role of law centres into the 1990s and beyond. I provide a broad outline of the principles and organizational structure that should inform any future national network of these innovative and valuable agencies, which do so much to provide effective access to legal advice and assistance for those who would otherwise be legally indigent.

My interest in law centres began when I was a postgraduate student at Nuffield College, Oxford, where I was fortunate to receive much valuable advice from A.H.Halsey. My good fortune did not end there, however, for my university supervisor, Keith Hawkins, was extremely diligent and patient in helping me to develop my ideas. I owe them both an intellectual debt of gratitude, but more so I valued their friendly and kindly interest in me and my work. Over the years I have received generous assistance from a large number of law centres whose staff, despite the enormous pressure under which many of them work, have always found time to answer my enquiries.

Various friends have helped me directly in bringing this project to its conclusion, or have taken an encouraging interest in it. Accordingly, while taking sole responsibility for any failings in the text, I should like to thank the following: Ian and Liz Aston, Robin Barrow, Susan Bissegger, Allen Callaghan, Richard and Diane Cherry, Wendy Clark, Peter Golding, Arthur Gould, Witek Kowalski, David and Christine Russell, Jack Street, and Allan and Julia Tombs. In particular, I must thank Derek Edwards who was so generous with his time in explaining to me the intricacies of a new word processing system and in helping to print the final manuscript. Finally, let me mention the students, too numerous to name, whom I have taught in recent years. One of the reasons for writing this book was for their benefit, in the sense that I have tried to produce a clear and comprehensive account of the British law centre movement. I hope they think it has been worth it!

Loughborough
March 1990

1 Law centres, access to legal services, and citizenship

Law centres have emerged in relatively recent times to comprise an important sector in the delivery of legal services, which focuses on the areas of welfare and 'poverty' law. Despite the fact that law centres only number sixty agencies spread throughout the country, they have had an enormous impact on civil law and on the delivery of legal services in England and Wales. They have clearly demonstrated that a professional, *salaried* service can be organized to provide much – needed advice and representation to poor and working – class individuals. They have shown too that law centres can not only acquire thorough expertise in the poverty law areas, but can also take the lead in trying to use the law in ways that will allow their clients to enjoy their legal rights. In short, law centres have provided a new form of access to legal services in England and Wales and, through the services they supply, they are attempting to realize what might be termed the rights associated with citizenship. But what does the concept of citizenship mean in this context?

The Concept Of Citizenship

Citizenship is a value – concept in the sense that in a democratic society our understanding of the term is intimately bound up with the changing nature of society's values. Out of the ebb and flow of social debate, the development of social policies, and the actual provision of social welfare, there emerges a set of obligations and rights by which we broadly attach meaning to the term 'citizenship'. The meaning of citizenship is subject to the push and pull of

1

various forces and it may change over time. For instance, the version of citizenship inspired by the Beveridge Report during the Second World War, and given concrete shape in the late 1940s and early 1950s, was based on the idea that the state should provide minimum standards of welfare and income maintenance for its citizens. However, current ideas on the centralized provision of social welfare have shifted somewhat from the focus on state delivery towards encouraging individuals and families to provide more for themselves.

I am not suggesting one version is better than the other; only that both are value – laden. Moreover, it is clear that there is no single route to the realization of citizenship rights. This holds true also in the area of the delivery of legal services and of their relationship to the realization of citizenship rights. Citizens may seek to realize their legal rights – an element of citizenship – in a variety of ways. In the law centre context, however, only two ways are available. On the one hand, there is the reactive delivery of legal services, often associated with a 'bureaucratic' approach and, on the other hand, there is the proactive delivery mechanism, often associated with a more 'participatory' style. Reactive and proactive are concepts that I shall explain in detail in the following chapter, while the bureaucratic and participatory approaches will be explained shortly. Before that, however, I shall deal with the idea of citizenship and its relationship to legal services.

Citizenship, Legal Services and Institutional Access

T.H.Marshall (1976:72) posited three basic elements to the concept of citizenship; political, social, and civil. The political element was 'the right to participate in the exercise of political power, as a member of a body invested with political authority or as an elector of the members of such a body'. Parliament and local councils are the most relevant bodies here. Few citizens, however, become elected representatives and the vast majority participate in the exercise of political power only through the vote. A great deal of authority is invested in elected representatives, but the corollary of this is that when the citizen has cast his vote he then plays a relatively passive role: he is to be the recipient of policies and benefits decided by the elected representatives, and is not expected, on the whole, to play a role in actively formulating them.

The social element of citizenship covered the right of citizens to enjoy minimum standards of welfare and security, and the institutions most closely associated with it are education, social security, and social services. This element is supposed to alleviate the social and economic chasm between the 'haves' and the 'have – nots' by postulating the right of everyone to enjoy a minimum standard of living compatible with a civilized existence according to the criteria of the day. Writing in the late 1940s, Marshall's original analysis was based on the idea of state provision of such services. This service delivery model was essentially centralized and bureaucratic in its approach. It allowed for comprehensive coverage and equity among recipients of the services, although in reality these goals have not always been achieved. What such an approach does not seek to achieve is the active participation of citizens in the formulation, development, and management of social welfare policies.

A centralized and bureaucratic approach aims to supply the public with appropriate services and benefits, but the policy – making process affecting these services and benefits is largely remote from the citizen. As Hadley and Hatch (1981:22) have noted, it provides 'no opportunities for direct public involvement in the management of services...' The public – the consumers – are relatively passive recipients. This is not necessarily to insist that they ought to be involved; it is simply to point out that on the whole the citizenship rights that the public enjoy are not the product of active citizen participation. Indeed, in the period after the Second World War neither Marshall, nor the majority of citizens, saw participation as a necessary and valuable component of the policy – making process. For many citizens simply being allocated services and benefits and being in receipt of them were sufficient. In this sense the bureaucratic delivery mechanism is perfectly acceptable; but there are also benefits of a different kind associated with the participatory approach, which should not be overlooked. Such issues resurface in Marshall's third element of citizenship; the civil component.

Marshall (1976:71) defined the civil element as being

> composed of the rights necessary for individual freedom – liberty of the person, freedom of speech, thought and faith, the right to own property and to conclude valid contracts and the right to justice. The last is of a different order from the others because it is the right to defend and assert all one's rights on terms of equality with others and by due process of law. This shows us that the institutions most directly associated with civil rights are the courts of justice.

In his discussion of the civil element Marshall again emphasized the importance of access to appropriate institutions. A blockage of access could, therefore, undermine attempts to realize citizenship rights. So far as Marshall was concerned most of the blockages to the first two elements of citizenship had been removed by the provision of compulsory state education, the introduction of income – maintenance policies and means – testing for those in need, the adoption of the universal adult franchise, and the remuneration of Members of Parliament, thereby alleviating the necessity for a private income. But obstacles to the realization of the civil element were not so easily overcome in Marshall's view, for litigation, unlike voting, is an expensive business.

Marshall was aware that without adequate access to justice rights recognized in principle might not be enjoyed in practice. Accordingly, he traced three major attempts to overcome the blockages associated with the right to justice. First, there had been the establishment in 1846 of county courts to provide in civil cases

3

'cheap justice for the common people'. However, even here costs were not negligible and the county court's jurisdiction was limited. Second, there had been the development of a poor person's procedure under which a small fraction of the poor could sue, *in forma pauperis*, free of nearly all cost with the voluntary assistance of members of the legal profession. Unfortunately, eligibility was so restrictive that the procedure became mainly limited to matrimonial cases. Third, Marshall saw the enactment of the 1949 Legal Aid and Advice Bill as a bold measure to increase access to justice. One can also add subsequent similar acts, and the development of small claims courts and tribunals as further measures to open up access to justice.

In extending the capabilities of the courts in these various ways to serve more effectively the needs of indigent citizens, there has been an obvious increase in access. But there are three caveats to be considered. First, while tribunals are an important adjudication forum, Legal Aid is not normally available for those appearing before them. Second, small claims courts still have their limitations and are as likely to be used against poor people by debt collectors as by the indigent themselves. Third, the Legal Aid system itself is subject to a number of problems, chiefly concerning its complexity and financial eligibility criteria that combine to lessen its effectiveness as a mechanism for pressing the claims of low – income individuals.

Law centres are the most recent development that may be added to the list of innovations designed to open up access to justice. The first law centre in Britain began work in 1970 and since then they have tended to locate themselves in deprived, inner – city areas. Usually their services are free, and the centres are funded by a combination of charitable and public monies. This allows them to employ salaried lawyers who specialize in areas most relevant to their clients, such as housing, welfare, and employment law. Normally, law centres are sited in highly visible and accessible locations, and they remain open for long hours including some evening and weekend periods. These characteristics, combined with a relaxed and informal atmosphere within the centres, have helped them to increase significantly access to justice for their predominantly low – income clients.

To Marshall the essential elements of citizenship could only be realized when there was sufficient access to the appropriate institutions on which fulfilment of the various elements depended. But access alone is not a guarantee of the realization of the rights of citizenship. The non – take – up of welfare benefits, particularly Income Support benefits, is just one well – known example. One cannot equate access with universal usage, for in the legal field many potential clients may not realize that they have a legal problem or claim. Citizenship, therefore, does not depend on access alone; it also depends on the individual actively seeking to exercise his rights of citizenship. This idea of the active citizen returns me to a discussion of the two models for the delivery of social welfare and legal services.

The Participatory And Bureaucratic Delivery Mechanisms

The manner in which citizenship rights are attained is dependent on two factors: objectively available access to relevant institutions of service, and the extent to which citizens are either actively or passively involved in securing the rights and benefits associated with those institutions. Each of those institutions, which include law centres, has its own service delivery mechanism. This mechanism may be described in ideal – type terms as either the participatory or the bureaucratic approach. Naturally, most institutions will have some combination of the two approaches, but a few may tend very strongly towards one end of the ideal – type continuum. For instance, it is difficult to see the country's defence forces being run on participatory lines with the public deciding on which ships, etc., should be sent where. That is not to deny the public does not have an interest in defence policies, only that it has no say in the day – to – day management of the armed services. However, the prospects for a more participatory approach in other areas, such as in the delivery of social welfare and legal services, may be more encouraging. Before commenting on the possible advantages of such an approach, I shall outline the characteristics of the bureaucratic delivery mechanism.

The Bureaucratic Approach

This style of delivery mechanism is designed to allow the efficient and rational distribution of scarce resources on the basis of equity, so that all citizens will receive their entitlements irrespective of social class or geographical considerations. In this way, the provision of welfare and other benefits has been massively extended throughout the UK and has had a significant impact on the lives of citizens. Despite this achievement, Hadley and Hatch (1981:23 – 31) have identified four major criticisms of the bureaucratic approach.

First, although bureaucratic officials are supposed to comply with the goals set out by their political masters, in practice there is a range of professional interests within bureaucracies that may modify compliance with those goals. It may be that those professional interests become pursued as ends in themselves, sometimes to the detriment of the officially recognized goals.

Second, contrary to the notion that bureaucracies are efficient and effective in the distribution of welfare resources, is the idea that they are often insufficiently accountable and uncompetitive. Coupled with substantial job security, this may lead to inertia and to a failure to maintain satisfactory levels of performance.

Third, bureaucracies responsible for social welfare policies have been slow to involve their own employees in decision – making, which has resulted in those institutions becoming innately conservative and resistant to change.

Fourth, according to Hadley and Hatch (1981:29), 'the exclusion of citizens from direct participation is particularly costly in terms of resources foregone and the potential for creating more responsive services'. The sheer scale of the public bureaucracies makes citizen participation problematic. The whole process of administrative rationalization and the use of managerial techniques have widened the gap between the provider of the service and the consumer in terms of the potential for citizen participation.

It can be argued that the complexity of modern government demands a bureaucratic style of administration and that despite the criticisms the system does work tolerably well in practice. The supporters of the participatory approach would argue that the costs of centralization and rationalization are too high, and that what is required is to organize social welfare services on a local basis to ensure that services are responsive and accountable. It may be that here the participatory model is flawed in that the local control and delivery of welfare policies – based on inputs from the local populace – may apply only to a limited range of services. Moreover, local provision may also lead to variations in the quality and quantity of services that would be unacceptable.

The Participatory Approach

In the participatory model the general directions of social welfare policy are still laid down by central government, but their development and precise implementation are subject to negotiation between agency staff and local consumers. A participatory institution or agency has wider terms of reference than a bureaucratic one, and it encourages a cooperative approach between itself and the consumers of its services. Under the bureaucratic model authority is located within the organizational hierarchy, but in the participatory model this is only one aspect of authority. In addition to authority being based on formal position and on professional qualifications, the participatory agency also acknowledges the worth of the practical experience and the position in the community of its clientele. Furthermore, unlike the relatively well–defined roles of staff in a bureaucratic institution, the roles in a participatory agency are more flexible, and there is an expectation that clients will adopt an active posture in relationships with staff. This interaction of staff and consumers is supposed to produce a more innovatory organization since the interaction generates not only ideas for change, but also encourages the development of more self–reliant and competent consumers.

In a participatory model the concern for objective factors of performance, such as the number of cases processed, is accompanied by a desire to satisfy the expressed priorities of the agency's consumers. In this sense, accountability is supposed to be a two–way process in which the staff are accountable both to their formal employers and to their consumers or clients. Finally, the participatory model suggests that professional staff recognize not only their own expert knowledge, but also value the knowledge of the lay – person with whom they are prepared to work in partnership.

Hadley and Hatch (1981:86) argue that the participatory model identifies the capacity of clients to become self – reliant, and they note that citizen participation is an essential strategy in increasing the responsiveness of agencies' services to local conditions. Moreover, this approach draws on the resources of the community and its inhabitants, which under the bureaucratic model remain largely untapped. Inherent, therefore, in the participatory model is the claim that the active involvement of the client in the development and management of services leads to the citizen directly influencing the nature of his citizenship rights. Moreover, a further claim is made that active participation not only provides tangible benefits for clients, but also that it encourages the development of more self – reliant and competent individuals. The pros and cons of the bureaucratic and participatory approaches, in relation to the actual work of law centres, will be discussed in subsequent chapters. First, however, I shall cover the notion that the active exercise of citizenship rights leads to greater individual competence.

Active Citizenship, Participation And Competence

Marshall's original analysis of citizenship was based on the idea of objective access to the relevant bodies. His later writings, however, are somewhat different and he placed greater emphasis on the participatory approach in which citizens are subjectively aware of the broad characteristics of civil rights and of the power that potentially inheres within them (Marshall, 1981b:137 – 53). Whereas social rights relate to citizens, for the most part, as consumers of benefits bestowed on them by the state, the pursuit of civil rights potentially casts the citizen in the role of actor. These civil rights are so basic and fundamental to citizens that they are the expression of

> principles which are internalised in the early stages of socialisation. They thus become part of the individual's personality, a pervasive element in his daily life, an intrinsic component of his culture, the foundation of his capacity to act socially and the creator of the environmental conditions which make social action possible in a democratic civilisation (Marshall, 1981b:141).

Marshall(1981b:145) argued that civil rights were a form of power that offered the capacity for citizen action and were closely linked to the development of citizen competence.

However, while the social institution, which we call civil rights, is well – established in the UK, that is not to say that all citizens enjoy equal opportunities to avail themselves of its potential benefits. When Halsey (1984:14) refers to civil rights as constituting a culture, he distinguishes between a general cultural awareness among the

7

citizenry concerning the merits of the right to justice, and the varying opportunities of individual citizens to pursue strategies devoted to that end. Here lies an important role for law centres. We can assume that there is a culture of civil rights, but we cannot assume that public awareness of this culture is necessarily or easily translated into concrete action.

Citizens may, for instance, be unaware that they have a specific legal claim. Moreover, even if they do recognize a claim, they may still fail to identify an appropriate agency to which to take the claim. These problems rarely exist when the legal issue is, for example, conveyancing for most people will recognize their legal need and identify a private solicitor as the person who can meet this need for conveyancing. However, the recognition of a legal claim or need and the identification of an appropriate agency may not be so readily conceived in respect of other issues, such as tenancy disputes and welfare entitlements. Law centres have played an important role here by advertizing their services, thereby helping working – class individuals to recognize their legal claims and to identify law centres as relevant institutions of service. It is within a broad social framework of the culture of civil rights that citizens take various forms of action through which to secure the rights of citizenship. But if some citizens cannot gain access to relevant agencies then their abilities to pursue their rights are curtailed. Law centres have extended the number of citizens who can now take specific action in respect of their rights. In short, law centres attempt to meet unmet legal needs, and the manner in which they provide access to legal services is, in effect, to operationalize Marshall's concept of the right to justice, the most important component of the civil element of citizenship.

Whereas Marshall saw justice mainly in terms of legal processes and remedies[1], Galanter's (1976:225 – 6) notion of access to *legality* has a wider relevance. Legal claims need not only be pursued in the courtroom, but also in negotiations with other kinds of institutions. In this sense, Galanter's concept of legality is more diffuse than Marshall's notion of justice, since the former requires not only appropriate expertise within the courts, but also 'the ability, knowledge and confidence to handle public bureaucracies' (Parker, 1979:33). Some law centres have been particularly innovative in pursuing strategies in areas beyond the courts, and they have pioneered a combination of legal and non – legal avenues of action for the redress of clients' grievances. Thus, in addition to operationalizing Marshall's concept of access to justice, they have also gone some way to making a reality of Galanter's ideas on access to legality.

Access to legality includes not only the notion of gaining benefits through winning one's case in court, but also of securing the accountability of officials, and of the participation of individuals in decisions that will affect their own lives (Galanter, 1976:225 – 6). Of course, this is also one of the aims of the participatory model discussed earlier. Within that model consumer or client participation was closely associated with the development of client competence, and to the extent that law centres encourage the active involvement of clients in pursuing their rights, they too are linked with the idea of enhancing client capability. But why is the concept of client competence so important, and what are its alleged benefits?

All law centres pursue legal action, which, according to Nonet (1971:53), embodies

values that are closely connected with the values of citizenship and political participation in a democracy. One of the things that is involved in legal action is self – assertion, affirming the legitimacy of one's interests, and seeking recognition of one's claims...The legal actor is one who resists the blind pursuit of self interest and the direct use of power, and seeks to appeal to the authority of general standards in support of what he claims. Yet a third characteristic that is present, however, is the criticism of authority, holding officials accountable to rules, compelling them to respond to claims and arguments, to justify themselves. These are some of the latent values that are implicit even in the most routine forms of legal action.

Nonet refers to the legally competent actor as someone who is self – assertive and transforms his problem into an issue of principle. A person who has identified a grievance and taken it to a law centre for advice and assistance may be said to be acting in a legally competent manner.

However, the competence of citizens to identify and to act on their problems need not be seen in a one – dimensional fashion. As Nonet (1971:55) argues: 'there are important continuities between legal and political action, in that both embody similar sorts of values, such as self – assertion, criticism of authority, reductions of power...' The competence embodied in the ability to pursue legal action is similar to that embodied in the pursuit of political action. I do not assume, however, that the development of legal competence leads automatically to the emergence of political competence among individuals. It will depend on circumstances. For example, where an otherwise legally competent citizen pursues his claim in a routine fashion using normal legal tactics and forums, the link between legal and political competence may be weak. That is not to say that the legal competence exhibited is of no practical relevance. Given the similarity between the two forms of competence, it is likely to be the manner in which the claim is pursued that will influence the kind of competence that emerges. However, is this saying nothing more than there is no difference between the two? That it is only a question of applying different labels to what is substantially the same kind of behaviour? I think not.

The legally competent actor is operating in a relatively circumscribed environment. There are certain expected procedures, certain roles to follow, and only certain outcomes are possible. The citizen pursuing political action in a competent fashion inhabits an environment with the potential for greater variety of tactics to be adopted; the outcomes are also more numerous and perhaps less certainly known. Furthermore, the potential for generalized lessons to be learned from specific claims involving the pursuit of political action may be greater. Thus, one might expect the politically competent law centre client subsequently to exhibit this competence in settings other than that in which the original claim was pursued. In other words, the development of political competence might reasonably be expected to have a spillover effect on the lives of law centre clients in a variety of other situations. The issue of legal and political competence will be discussed further in later chapters when I provide empirical evidence on the work of law centres.

Our understanding of citizenship and the meaning we attach to it are still evolving in today's society. Pinker, for instance, while fearful that many citizens may become dependent upon professionals and professional expertise, takes the view that the 'enjoyment of citizenship is synonymous with its exercise' (Pinker, 1979:140 – 1). Parker's perspective on citizenship builds on the idea of exercising one's rights. She argues that citizenship must also emphasize

the right to take part in the planning of services which vitally affect people's lives and in decisions which do not call for some kind of professional or expert knowledge not possessed by the layman. Similarly, it carries the right of enquiry into and criticism of customary forms of provision or administrative procedures.

The crucial problem here is to distinguish those kinds of decision which should be left to the professionals or officials because they depend on a body of skill, experience or specialised knowledge which the layman or ordinary consumer does not have, and those in which the consumer should take part because he is the only 'expert' available. Or to put it another way, it is a problem of deciding how far and in what circumstances the professional's claim to know best what is good for other people may be justified (Parker, 1979:153).

Whatever meaning one attaches to the concept of citizenship the role of the citizen himself is vital. One of the most important aspects of the citizen's role is the extent to which he is either a passive recipient of benefits and services associated with citizenship, or he is actively involved in influencing the nature of those benefits and engaged in the management of those services. So far as legal services and benefits are concerned the extent of citizen participation is heavily influenced by the manner in which the claim is initiated; the manner in which the law is mobilized. Many of the ideas and themes discussed in this chapter will surface again later in the book, but now I turn my attention to the mobilization of law and to the nature of the lawyer – client relationship.

Notes

1.   On this issue of claims being identified as legal problems, Morris (1973:54, Original italics) has argued that:
     The disprivileged *themselves* tend to recognize as legal problems only the traditional ones, so that a vicious circle emerges, where the law does not do much about social change unless it is in the interests of its own class, nor do the poor make *demands* in this direction.

2 The mobilization of law and the nature of the lawyer–client relationship

The Reactive And Proactive Mobilization Of Law

The process of civil law does not automatically swing into action, *deus ex machina*, to fight injustice; it has to be set in motion by an active party. Black refers to the manner in which the legal process is set in motion as the mobilization of law. According to Black (1973:128, Original italics):

> A case can enter a legal system from two possible directions. A citizen may set the legal process in motion by bringing a complaint; or the state may initiate a complaint on its own authority, with no participation of a citizen complainant. In the first sequence a legal agency reacts to a citizen, so we refer to it as a *reactive* mobilization process. In the second sequence, where a legal official acts with no prompting from a citizen, we may speak of a *proactive* mobilization process.

The concepts of reactivity and proactivity are, in effect, ideal–types, which may apply to a number of institutions, not simply to legal agencies. Thus, a patient visiting his general practitioner about an ailment may be seen as a reactive utilization of the health care system: it is the individual who sets in motion the treatment process. In contrast, the work of the School Medical Service and of immunization and 'screening' programmes are largely proactive initiatives carried out by health care agencies that offer their respective services for the public's benefit. Various segments of the public are defined by these agencies as being in need of the services they provide. In respect of law centres, a client

12

approaching his local centre with, for instance, a social security issue would be mobilizing the legal process in a reactive manner. However, where staff at the law centre identify a problem, for example one that is common to a number of citizens within the neighbourhood, and then take various forms of action to try to solve that problem, a proactive mobilization of the law has taken place. A further example of a proactive endeavour would be community – based educational projects designed to increase people's awareness of their legal rights.

While Black's formulation could apply to many agencies, the concepts of reactivity and proactivity have a crucial bearing upon both the nature and the impact of the legal services provided by community law centres. The manner in which the law is mobilized influences the way citizens realize their rights. If a citizen is to take the initiative and to register details with a law centre about a possible legal complaint, it follows that the individual must be able to gain relatively easy access to the agency in question. Reactive law centres, therefore, have an open – door policy, which allows citizens to pursue in an effective manner their awareness that they may have a legal complaint. Each individual citizen coming into the law centre will be seen on a one – to – one basis by a member of the law centre staff.

Although there are other consequences, which stem from the operation of a reactive law centre, one of the most important is the creation and implementation of an individualized lawyer – client relationship. Such a relationship is different from that which can exist within a proactive law centre, where much work is *group orientated*, and I shall be exploring that difference shortly.

Moreover, since a reactive centre relies for the most part on citizen – initiated complaints, it may not always enjoy an accurate or comprehensive understanding of the range of legal issues affecting people within its catchment area. Potential clients of the law centre may not present themselves because they choose to ignore the legal problem confronting them, or they may feel (rightly or wrongly) that the law centre can do little or nothing to alleviate it, or else they may be unaware that they have a legal grievance that may be pursued by the law centre. Of course, there are several ways in which a reactive law centre can help to overcome any deficiency in its understanding of the range of legal problems afflicting its potential clientele – such as by conducting community – based research and by having a management committee largely composed of local people – but the essential point is that the services it provides are predominantly those dictated by the problems of clients who present themselves at the law centre. However, when individuals have decided to come to the law centre such a reactive agency can usually count upon those individuals to provide detailed information about their own respective problems.

Another consequence of the reactive mobilization of law, according to Black, is that it is essentially a conservative mechanism. He bases this argument on the observation that the tendency of

13

citizens is to use the law only as a last resort, and thus the status quo is left largely intact. There is some support for this view, especially in the light of working – class groups that may be wary of the cost of using the law and deterred from approaching private solicitors because of their image and the often relative inaccessibility of their offices. However, the advent of law centres has led to the development of new areas of legal expertise in the field of welfare law. This has meant that for many working – class people the creation of a law centre in their locality has offered greater opportunity to initiate complaints. On the one hand, a high level of citizen – initiated complaints provides the potential for altering the status quo and improving the socio – economic environment of working – class clients as they pursue their legal rights. On the other hand, too high a level of individual cases within reactive law centres might place heavy burdens on the individualized lawyer – client relationship with a corresponding fall in the quality of law centre services.

Black (1973: 134 – 5) also argues that

reactive systems operate on a case – by – case basis. Cases enter the system one by one, and they are processed one by one. This creates an intelligence gap about the relations among and between cases. It is difficult to link patterns of illegal behavior to single or similar violators and thus to deal with the sources rather than merely the symptoms of these patterns. To discover these patterns a systematic search for factual similarities across cases is needed.

This would be true if any agency were operating in a wholly reactive manner. Reactivity and proactivity may be seen as ideal – types at either end of a reactive – proactive continuum. While it is true that most reactive law centres are firmly located towards the reactive end of the continuum, that is not to say that all cases or activities are carried out on a case – by – case basis. A minor proactive emphasis within a predominantly reactive law centre may modify some of the centre's operations. For instance, a commitment to community – based research would help the centre to discover the patterns of legal problems within the catchment area, which may not be obvious to the various law centre staff who are processing their own discrete batches of individual cases. Moreover, a centre may identify some issues as having a common relevance to a number of individual cases, and may decide to try to solve such issues by adopting a group or collective approach. Finally, a reactive centre may conduct local educational campaigns to increase people's legal awareness and even to encourage them to take forms of self – help action to solve their problems. However, where a reactive law centre is simply overwhelmed with individual cases, although there may be an organizational desire to alter this state of affairs, it may be impossible to do little other than to process the cases individually. Whether these events take place, and to what extent reactive law centres can modify their heavily reactive style of operation, are empirical issues that I shall be addressing in later chapters.

There are also consequences that stem from the proactive mobilization of law. For instance, Black (1973:137) argues that in contrast to the reactive mobilization of law the proactive approach 'can deal with patterns rather than mere instances of illegality, which gives it a strong preventive capacity...' However, in order to deal with those patterns a proactive law centre must first be able to recognise them. This can be achieved in the same way as reactive law centres: namely, through community – based forms of research and a management committee of local people who can give information about the nature of legal problems in the area. Once again, the extent to which proactive law centres pursue such activities is an empirical issue, which will be explored in later chapters.

Even if one assumes that a proactive law centre does possess an accurate overview of the legal and other problems existing within its catchment area, the question of which problems become issues for law centre action still remains. Whereas Black (1973:138) views the reactive mobilization of law as the legal equivalent of the market economy in which individual citizens rationally and voluntarily pursue their own interests, the proactive mobilization he likens to a social welfare model of law. In the ideal – type, pure, form of proactive mobilization the legal good of the citizenry is decided upon by the government, and the citizens have no direct role in formulating such policies. In the reality of a modern democratic state, such a situation would raise serious ethical problems. Moreover, in practice, citizens do play some role, albeit often minor, in formulating legal and social policy. As far as law centres are concerned, and particularly proactive centres, the opportunities for citizens/clients to become involved in policy formation are in theory much greater.

This participatory potential stems from two sources. First, the role of clients as members of management committees who set policy goals for law centres is a possible avenue of citizen participation. This would apply to both reactive and proactive centres. Second, the ability of client groups working with proactive law centres to alleviate a problem common to their individual members is another potentially important influence on the manner in which their collective cases are pursued. According to Black, a proactive agency makes up its own organizational mind about what activities to pursue in the public interest. Law centres, however, offer scope for modifying this theoretical position. Moreover, although I have yet to deal with the subject of lawyer – client relations in detail, proactive law centres by virtue of the special nature of the relationship between client – group and law centre staff offer even greater potential for citizen participation in formulating the law centres' policies and choice of activities. Client participation in pursuing legal rights and the rights associated with citizenship will be a recurring theme throughout this book.

Reactivity and proactivity are essentially forms of mediation between the law and the legal problems that citizens encounter; they are in effect broad but different strategies of representation. Whereas the work of reactive law centres may be heavily influenced both by the nature of the legal categories and problems that individuals take to these agencies, and by the sheer number of cases, the approach of proactive law centres may also be influenced by the organizational capacities and competences of the client groups with which they are in contact (Mayhew, 1975:414). Each form of representation has implications for the manner in which clients attempt to realize the rights of citizenship. Moreover, the manner in which professional practitioners operate within a largely reactive or a proactive law centre context has further consequences for the realization of citizenship rights and for the participatory role of clients themselves. Before arriving at an in–depth consideration of the role of law centre lawyers – I shall use the term 'lawyers' to refer to both solicitors and barristers – I must first outline some of the details of law centre operations.

Law Centres: The Record Of Achievement

The nature of lawyer–client relations cannot be fully assessed without first describing the work and achievements of British law centres. The development of law centres has been both a recognition that the rights of low–income people to enjoy access to legal advice and assistance were inadequate, and a tangible opportunity for such citizens to pursue their claims more vigorously in the area of poverty law. There are a number of essential ingredients in the organization and operation of law centres that deserve specific mention. They include: meeting unmet need in particular geographical locations; offering what is normally a free and non–stigmatizing service; developing areas of expertise; and expanding the potential for a more participatory method of service delivery, which involves the concept of consumer control. I shall now deal with these more fully.

Unmet Legal Need

The satisfaction of unmet legal need depends both on client demand – an awareness of a legal claim, determination to pursue it, and knowledge of whom to approach – and on the physical availability and accessibility of relevant institutions. Law centres stimulate client demand by siting themselves, in the main, in inner–city locations of high visibility and convenience close to or along main thoroughfares. Their premises are usually open not only during normal office hours but also for periods during the evening and weekend so that their low–income clients need not lose time and pay from work in order to visit the centres. The atmosphere in law centres is normally relaxed, non–intimidating, and informal. Wherever possible services are given free of charge. Private practitioners, in contrast, have more restrictive office hours, a more formal style, and are not located in large numbers within inner – city areas[1].

Little systematic information is available on the location of private solicitors' offices, but Foster's (1973: 153 – 66) study gives some indication of their relative under – representation in inner – city areas. In his analysis of municipal, county, and London boroughs in England and Wales in which population per solicitor was calculated, Foster listed all 184 boroughs in rank order. First was Bournemouth with one solicitor for every 913 of the population. However, in 142nd place, for example, was Brent with one solicitor per 5,694 residents, and in 154th place was Wandsworth with 6,449 people per practitioner. In Tower Hamlets there were 16,499 people per solicitor's office. Clearly the location of many law centres in inner – city areas was a valuable response to unmet legal need and an important attempt to widen access to legal services.

A Free and Non – Stigmatizing Service

Client demand is further enhanced by the fact that law centres try to provide as many services as possible free of charge to their consumers. Clients eligible for Legal Aid are not always subject to strict investigation of their financial means, and some centres have waived clients' contributions to the costs of legally – aided cases. At the very least, law centre staff aim to provide free advice to an individual, or to refer the client to another more appropriate agency if the centre cannot handle the case itself. Moreover, since law centres receive public monies and their lawyers are salaried, they can provide advice and take on cases requiring detailed attention without thought for the cash nexus that joins private solicitors to their clients. Having salaried lawyers in law centres means that the ability of the client to pay for the service he receives is no longer a crucial factor. Law centre staff do not need therefore to undertake rigorous means – testing of all clients and, in turn, this means that a potential source of stigma is removed. Moreover, since most law centre funds come from local and central government, the service they provide is not necessarily seen by clients as a charitable one. On the contrary, it is a service available to inhabitants of specific catchment areas, which in part is paid for by the tax and rate payers of those areas.

There is, however, one final sense in which the services of a law centre are not stigmatizing. The problems that poor people bring to law centres are treated with legitimacy and are seen as important grievances. In short, clients are treated as having a right to enjoy legal advice and assistance.

Legal and Non – Legal Expertise

Poor people and low – income groups typically have problems in the fields of housing tenancy and repair, employment, and welfare entitlements. There are several agencies dealing with such problems but few of them have the ability of law centres to pursue strategic legal (and occasionally non – legal) avenues for their solution. Housing Aid Centres may refer a client to a private solicitor as may Citizens Advice Bureaux; a trade unionist may get help from a solicitor appointed or employed by his own union; but none of these agencies are law centres, which specialize in all the main legal areas of complaint common among poor people. In this sense, law centres have become an 'institution' of expert service in the relatively new area of poverty law.

Moreover, law centres are not simply confined to pursuing legal avenues of advice and action; they may sometimes engage in non – legal strategies. These non – legal activities can be a most useful adjunct to the more traditional legal ones, and they may involve law centre staff in working closely with local inhabitants on issue – campaigns and with local organized groups to further collective interests. Proactive law centres are more heavily committed to such work than their reactive counterparts.

Participation and Consumer Control

In principle, there is potential in the operation of law centres for clients to become involved both in the general management of the centres and in the processing of their respective cases, whether these be individual or group cases. Indeed, this idea of consumer control has enjoyed a large measure of support over the years from individual law centres[2] and from the Law Centres' Federation[3], which has argued (1977:47) that each law centre should have a management committee composed of representatives from the local community. Such a composition, it is thought, helps to ensure that a law centre will continue to respond sensitively and efficiently to local need and thereby prevent the domination of professional interests in the running of the agency. Client participation in, or even control over, the management committee of a law centre is an interesting concept, but one that should not be viewed uncritically. As I shall argue later in this book, there have been a number of difficulties in making a reality of the concept of consumer control.

Equally, the notion of the client's active participation in the processing of his case must also be looked at with care, for it is easy to claim too much for this phenomenon. The original view of the Law Centres' Federation was that law centres ought to be devoting more resources towards encouraging clients to form their own organizations through which they could pursue collective solutions for their difficulties. While such a view may be seen as a goal towards which the law centre movement as a whole has been urged to move, in practice one must investigate each law centre in order to learn whether a significant level of client participation and control is being achieved. Such an investigation typically uncovers those factors that prevent law centres from making significant gains in this area.

18

The concept of consumer participation and control has important consequences for clients, whether they be individual clients or members of client groups. In respect of the latter, Newham Rights Centre (1974 – 5:42) argued that encouraging the formation of client groups to engage actively in seeking solutions to collective problems was not only a more efficient use of scarce resources, but also provided more opportunities to realize citizenship rights than was the case with the individual case – by – case approach. These opportunities included both legal and non – legal strategies. Furthermore if the legal awareness and competence of clients are to be enhanced through the groupwork approach, then the law centre staff must be at pains to explain to the group members the available courses of action and their likely consequences. Group members must also be encouraged to take responsibility for decision – making. Such an approach is in keeping with the participatory model and, indeed, may apply to individuals *qua* individuals as well as to group members. Whoever the client, this approach is supposed to encourage professionals not only to share their expert knowledge with clients, but also to recognize the worth of clients' own information that is relevant to the problems in hand. Such a process – an integral part of the lawyer – client relationship – has been called 'informed consent', and all law centres, in theory, have a commitment to providing high levels of informed consent.

However, the operationalization of informed consent is not uniform throughout the law centre movement. The biggest influence on levels of informed consent is whether a law centre operates predominantly in a reactive or a proactive fashion.

Conceptual Models Of The Reactive And Proactive Lawyer – Client Relationships

From the initial manner in which the law is mobilized – reactively or proactively – it is possible to outline two models of the reactive and proactive delivery of law centre services. These models are ideal – types. In reality no law centre would be wholly reactive or wholly proactive; rather it would have an operational philosophy and set of activities that tended towards one end of the reactivity – proactivity continuum. How law centres with a tendency towards either a reactive or a proactive style actually operate in relation to the following two conceptual models, and how their lawyer – client relationships conform to or depart from those models, will be discussed in detail in later chapters.

First, however, in order to construct these models consideration must be given to several key concepts, which are informed consent; party upgrading; client competence; people – working; and forms of occupational control.

Informed Consent

In a law centre with a bureaucratic approach the client would be expected to play an active role neither in the management of the centre nor in the actual processing of his case. In a centre with a participatory emphasis one would expect to find a more active involvement of consumers or clients. The basis for a cooperative, participatory relationship between professional and client in the legal sphere does exist. Rueschemeyer (1964) and Campbell (1976) have indicated that much of the work of the lawyer is founded on interpersonal skills rather than on wholly esoteric knowledge. Thus, there is ample opportunity for clients to contribute their own lay expertise. Indeed, Rosenthal in his study of personal injury cases found that

> many clients are capable of at least some degree of active participation in the process of making their claims and that active client participation correlates positively and significantly (statistically and analytically) with a good recovery (Rosenthal, 1976a:118).

The potential and ability of the client to participate in the disposition of his own case is a crucial aspect of the process of informed consent. The other aspect is the willingness and the skill of the professional in developing client participation. Rosenthal defined informed consent as a dialogue between lawyer and client, which ideally works as follows:

> The lawyer draws upon his or her expertise to set out for the client the possible ways to proceed. The estimated costs and anticipated benefits of the available choices are carefully reviewed. Where the lawyer deems it appropriate, he or she counsels the client as to the choices the lawyer thinks to be preferable, explaining why. Proper counselling, therefore, does not mean presenting the client with the one approach the lawyer prefers, but is a mutual process of joint exploration of options, in which the lawyer tries to be responsive to the concerns of the client and feels free to express his or her concerns as well. If it works, the clients weighs what has been discussed, chooses, and agrees to cooperate with the lawyer in pursuing the preferred strategy, or waives his right to choose by explicitly delegating the choice to the lawyer. Either way, the client authorizes the lawyer to proceed and shares the responsibility for the course of action taken... the process of informed consent is an unappreciated but essential part of competent performance. This is so not only because it enhances the dignity of the client, but because there is evidence it can actually increase the efficiency, the productiveness of the representation (Rosenthal, 1976b:271 – 2).

Rosenthal's use of the concept of informed consent highlights how the legal competence of clients might be developed. In theory, informed consent also applies to a range of non – legal solutions to a particular problem. This raises the potential that professional – client relationships exploring non – legal strategies might also encourage the growth of political competence among clients. The important dimension in both legal and political competence is the level and quality of the client's participatory relationship with the professional practitioner and the nature of his active involvement in the handling of his case. While informed consent, and legal and political competence may apply to individuals and to groups, party upgrading by its very nature is a concept only relevant to organized bodies.

Party Upgrading and Client Competence

Party upgrading encompasses the ideas of informed consent and client competences but only in relation to members of groups. The term was coined by Galanter who was concerned about legality and how citizens gained access to legality. Marshall's ideas on access to justice through the exercise of one's civil rights are subsumed in Galanter's concept of legality, for legality refers collectively to those distributive benefits that stem from access to law. They include: protection, security, remedies for a variety of grievances and claims, securing accountability of officials, participation in decision – making, employment of facilitative rules to accomplish specific purposes, provision of a framework for reliance, and feelings of justice or fairness (Galanter, 1976:225 – 6).

It is clear from this list that legality is closely related to the behaviour of competent citizens seeking to realize their rights. Moreover, while access to law may result in many if not all of the benefits of legality, it is not the only avenue available. For instance, access to other dispute – resolving or decision – making processes may equally result in the realization of some of the benefits of legality. Indeed, participation in decision – making itself may involve the business of local authority housing departments and other kinds of forums that are not strictly speaking judicial institutions. The ability to influence decisions taken in these non – judicial forums may be gained through both legal and non – legal means.

Access to legality is not, however, an automatic event for all citizens. According to Galanter access is variable, but may be improved by making alterations to one or more of the four main elements of the legal system. These elements are rules, courts, lawyers, and parties (Galanter, 1974:96). While improvements can be made in respect of the first three elements, in Galanter's view the greatest area for concern, and the area of greatest variability, is at the level of the parties. In short, lack of party capability is the crucial barrier to effective access to legality. Galanter points to the advantages in capability typically enjoyed by organizations, which are most often the 'repeat – players' in the legal system. That is to say, such organizations are regularly involved in processing their own legal claims. In contrast, individuals pursuing civil legal proceedings are usually 'one – shotters' whose involvement are isolated, one – off events (Galanter, 1974:97 – 104).

To Galanter, therefore, the biggest disparities in access to legality are not between rich and poor but between individuals and organizations. Thus, 'parties differ in their capacity to utilize legal services. What is routine and rational for an organization is monstrous for an individual' (Galanter, 1976:235).

In order to minimize the barriers to legality experienced by individual 'one – shot' parties, Galanter argues that these individuals should try to gain some of the advantages of the organizational 'repeat – players'. These advantages include the aggregation of claims and grievances, the ability to use advance intelligence and to structure the next transaction, the development of expertise and economies of scale, the opportunity to forge facilitative informal relations with other important and relevant institutional officials, the ability to deploy longer – run strategies and to share possible risks, and the possibility of enjoying greater credibility in the eyes of significant adversaries or potential allies (Galanter, 1976:232). In turn, these advantages may be pursued by organizing

> individuals into coherent groups that have the ability to act in a coordinated fashion, look out for their long – range interests, benefit from high grade legal services, employ long – run strategies, etc (Galanter, 1976:236).

Such groups may be trade unions, tenants' associations, or other kinds of interest groups. In short, individuals with common claims or grievances can form themselves into organized groups in order to 'upgrade' their party capacity and thereby their ability to pursue collective solutions. It is for these reasons that

> upgrading of party capacity holds the greatest promise for promoting access to legality. Party capability includes a range of personal capacities which can be summed up in the term 'competence': ability to perceive grievance, information about availability of remedies, psychic readiness to utilize them, ability to manage claims competently, seek and utilize appropriate help, etc (Galanter, 1976:230 – 1).

Galanter's perspective on competence need not be confined to legal competence. There is scope here for the development of political competence, depending on how a group chooses to pursue a solution to its collective problem. In any event, the very fact of group organization itself may have an impact on the development of client competences, not least because of the activities required to form and to sustain an organized coherent group. As Nonet (1969:114) argues:

> Organizational advocacy can thus come directly to grips with the administrative and political dimensions of legal rights, thereby allowing citizens a fuller and richer participation in the legal process. It emphasizes the significance of political resources for the accomplishment of legal competence.

The development of client competences, informed consent, and party upgrading are all matters that, in theory, law centres seek to achieve. But how are they to be achieved?

People – Working Techniques

One way of securing the above aims is a method known as 'people – working', which may be practised by both lawyers and non – lawyers though the lawyers rarely, if ever, receive any professional training in this sphere. Bennett and Hokenstad (1973:23) have described people – workers as catalysts who

> through the communication of information and sharing of insights, attempt to help the client help himself. They can be differentiated from those professions who use knowledge to help the client but do not share it with them...Because the people workers are concerned with the client's relationship to his environment and communicate knowledge about this relationship, this type of professional frequently finds his performance related to economic or social goals of clients.

This style of working appears to be more characteristic of the law centre movement than of private legal practice. Indeed, the Law Centres' Federation (1980:6) has argued that flexibility of approach, a combination of skills, and ability to communicate information clearly to clients are all required by law centre staff in order to forge constructive relations with clients and, in addition, to counterbalance what are seen as the inadequacies of many lawyers' training and professional backgrounds. The deployment of people – working skills is one way of helping to achieve these desired traits. In essence, people – working skills are a mechanism by which legal expertise may be more effectively delivered. In addition, the knowledge base of people – working tries to relate the problems of clients to their wider social context (Bennett and Hokenstad, 1973:22). Such an approach with its emphasis also upon methodological issues – the actual ways in which clients seek solutions for their problems – potentially allows law centres to explore with clients legal and non – legal strategies. Whatever strategy is chosen, people – working involves professionals working with clients and not simply for them. It requires that knowledge and resources are shared with clients in order to encourage the development of informed consent, competence, and party upgrading.

But why should professionals be inclined to operate in this manner? Whether people – working techniques are used within a law centre depends on the nature of control within that centre.

Professional and Communal Control

Johnson (1972:45 – 6) refers to three types of occupational control: collegiate and its sub – type professionalist; patronage and its sub – type communal control; and mediation, the most usual form of which Johnson takes to be state mediation. For our purposes the most relevant forms of control are professionalist and communal. Professionalist control exists where the lawyer 'defines the needs of the consumer and the manner in which these needs are catered for' (Johnson, 1972:45). This is symptomatic of the bureaucratic approach discussed in Chapter One. Under professionalist control the typical lawyer – client relationship is normally

a fiduciary, one – to – one relationship initiated by the client and terminated by the professional. Consumer choice, a major element in consumer control, is weakened under such conditions and made ineffective by virtue of the consumers' heterogeneity and individualization (Johnson, 1972:53).

Johnson did not deal with consumer control at length and I have, therefore, drawn out some of his ideas as he applied them to corporate patronage. Communal control exists where 'the consumer defines his own needs and the manner in which they are to be met' (Johnson, 1972:46). Put another way: 'Communal control refers to a situation where...a community organization imposes upon producers communal definitions of needs and practice' (Johnson, 1972:46). This form of control is most closely associated with the participatory approach within institutions. Writing specifically about corporate patronage Johnson refers to the incidence of 'housed' legal counsel employed by large companies. In an analogous manner in – house counsel may exist under a system of communal control where, for instance, a law centre acts as a community resource for local people to use as a locus of advice and assistance. Furthermore, just as in – house practitioners are expected to be socially acceptable to their patrons, so one finds some parallels with law centre staff and their clients. Although relatively few law centre staff share the same economic and social status as their working – class clients, nevertheless many staff identify with the problems in their respective catchment areas. Thus, as with 'housed' counsel, many law centre staff build up 'local knowledge and skills relevant to local demands...'(Johnson, 1972:68).

Johnson argues that under corporate patronage professional practitioners tend to be apolitical lest any expression of political views embarrass the patron. However, since many law centres (especially those adopting people – working techniques) are involved in trying to solve client problems that have a wider socio – economic dimension beyond that of each individual, it is often difficult for such centres not to enter into political activities.

Having highlighted the practical achievements of law centres, and having discussed some of the most important theoretical concepts that apply to their work, I am now in a position to finalize this conceptual elaboration of the lawyer – client relationship as it applies in a reactive and a proactive law centre.

The Reactive Route towards the Realization of Citizenship Rights

The services of a reactively oriented law centre are initiated by individual clients. Their claims are processed on a case – by – case basis and, typically, each client enjoys a one – to – one relationship with the law centre lawyer. When lawyer and client discuss together the nature of the legal claim, the options available and their probable consequences, then informed consent and legal competence among clients may be expected to be operationalized and developed. However, since reactive law centres tend to focus on the legal dimension of client problems, one would not expect to see the political competence of clients being encouraged. Moreover, because of this focus on the legal aspects of client grievances the exploration of non – legal strategies would similarly be underdeveloped. In addition, little or no party upgrading would take place since the vast majority of cases and clients are handled on an individual basis.

Agencies offering free services to lower – income groups are normally agencies upon which heavy consumer demands are made. In the case of reactive law centres these demands are serviced by lawyers whose traditional training and background emphasize one – to – one relationships with clients. There is a tendency for these relationships to be controlled by the professional and, where the professional has to cope with heavy demands on his time and resources, there is further pressure not to involve clients actively in the processing of their cases. Accordingly, the levels of people – working techniques are not extensive since these are essentially strategies employed to encourage active client participation. Where a law centre employs a reactive delivery mechanism combined with a bureaucratic ethos, the tendencies towards the professionalist control of the lawyer – client relationship and towards the existence of passive clients will be reinforced. If a more participatory approach can be successfully introduced into the operation of a reactive law centre – even though there are severe difficulties in doing so – there may be some movement towards achieving greater levels of communal control and active clients, albeit while for the most part still working with individual clients on a case – by – case basis.

The Proactive Path towards Citizenship Rights

A proactive law centre typically intervenes in its neighbourhood to seek solutions to what it perceives as collective problems. The emphasis is placed upon working with groups since this is seen as a more efficient and effective use of resources. When law centre staff and group members discuss together the nature of the claim, the options available and the probable consequences, then informed consent and client competence may be expected to be operationalized and developed. Since proactive law centres are involved in helping clients to form and to run their own organized groups, and since they also emphasize legal and non – legal strategies, the development of both legal and political competence may be expected. Indeed, there may even be some 'spillover' effect; that is to say, some members of organized groups as they grow in confidence and competence might pursue other activities and claims in settings different from that of the original. Moreover, since most cases are handled on a group basis one would expect party upgrading to occur.

In a proactive law centre there is a tendency for professionals to operate outside the 'traditional' sphere of one – to – one relationships controlled by the practitioner. The emphasis is on communal control and on the use of people – working strategies in order to encourage clients to play an active role in the processing of their claims and in the running of their organized groups. This participatory approach is expected to reinforce client activity.

In principle, a bureaucratic approach could be associated with a proactive delivery mechanism, but in practice it is confined to reactive law centres. In reactive centres the bureaucratic style may be seen as an equitable manner of distributing scarce resources to individual clients. That is to say, all clients of reactive centres are seen as having a right to legal advice and action, which does not depend on whether the individual is a member of an existing group or whether he has a claim that may be added to those of other clients and pursued on a collective basis.

Likewise, the participatory approach is associated with the proactive delivery mechanism. Proactive centres need to be flexible in order to seek out potential client groups and to encourage them to organize and to pursue collective solutions to their problems. These aims closely resemble those of the participatory approach. In addition, proactive law centre staff must work together as a team pooling their various expertise and also recognizing the knowledge and experience of lay people. This too is similar to elements within the participatory approach, as indeed are the notions of consumer accountability and the ability of client groups to become self – reliant.

The particular operational levels of reactivity and proactivity, and the extent of bureaucratic and participatory emphases, will vary in the case of each law centre. However, some of the most important factors influencing those variations can be identified as follows:

1. The initial organizational structure and operational philosophy of the law centre.

2. The impact of subsequent modifications to the centre's organization and operation as achieved by law centre staff and clientele. Important factors that may motivate attempts to introduce modifications are the areas of staff expertise, their levels of job satisfaction, and the views of clients about the quality of the law centre's services.

3. The level of funding and resources available to the law centre in relation to the demands made upon its services.

4. The nature of 'external' constraints that may modify the law centre's work, such as the views of the law centre's funding

body, the attitude of the Law Society, and changes in the law itself. In the following chapter I shall be exploring these four factors in detail when I look at the origins and development of the law centre movement. In later chapters I shall be discussing the issues raised in the conceptual elaboration of the lawyer – client relationship and how these operate in practice within reactive and proactive law centres.

Notes

1. Moreover, in addition to the problems of location and image surrounding private solicitors, several studies have noted the tendency for poor clients to receive less than satisfactory service from some private practitioners. In the USA Carlin (1962) and Ladinsky (1963) have highlighted the low quality service provided to poor clients by 'solo' lawyers. In Britain Podmore (1980:27) reported that lawyers in small practices are similarly inclined to provide lower quality service to poor clients. Even when poor clients are legally aided they do not always receive diligent and high – quality service. Carlin and Howard (1965) in America refer to the mass processing of such cases and a similar picture emerges from White's (1975) study of solicitors' firms in Birmingham. White found that many of the firms in his survey considered Legal Aid work to be profitable only if handled in volume. Cases were thus processed in a standardized manner wherever possible, and a high turnover was maintained 'at the risk of lowering the quality of the service provided' (White, 1975:245 – 6).

2. See, for instance, Adamsdown Community Trust (1978:62), Newham Rights Centre (1977:3), and Brent Community Law Centre (1975:4).

3. The Law Centres' Federation is composed currently of sixty law centres. It represents the interests of the law centre movement as a whole, and it carries out valuable functions in commenting on policy and legislative initiatives, conducting training and development work, and organizing conferences, etc.

3 Law on the doorstep: the origins of law centres

While the concept of law centres emanated from the Legal Services Program in the USA, the first published support in Britain for the creation of indigenous law centres along the lines of the American model came from Michael Zander (1966). The debate started by Zander, and to which he continued to be an influential contributor, concentrated on the inadequacies of the prevailing legal services for the public, and for the poor in particular. It was essentially a debate about access to the legal system and the associated extent of unmet legal needs. Moreover, the debate overlapped slightly that period in Britain from 1962 onwards that can be characterized as the 'rediscovery of poverty'. To some extent one can view the creation of the law centre movement in the late 1960s as a response by the 'liberal' or 'socially activist' segment of the legal profession to that rediscovery. Part of the government's response was the setting up of the Community Development Project in 1969, out of which subsequently grew a few law centre schemes.

Opposing Views: The Law Society Versus The Society Of Labour Lawyers

One of the most important contributions to the emerging debate on law centres came from the Society of Labour Lawyers. Another contribution came from the Law Society, an institution not only committed to ensuring the quality of legal services within Britain, but also to representing the interests of its members who are practising solicitors. The course of this debate – covering

September 1966 with the publication of Zander's article, December 1968 with the publication of *Justice for All* by the Society of Labour Lawyers, and July 1969 with the final response of the Law Society to the idea of law centres – highlighted two opposing views on the creation of this new venture in public legal services.

Zander's 1966 article, which welcomed the idea of law centres, led to an invitation from the Lord Chancellor's Advisory Committee to present his arguments in more detail. However, the Committee, which throughout the 1980s became a supporter of the work of law centres, at that time (June 1967) remained unconvinced of the need either to alter the existing Legal Aid scheme or to set up law centres. This attitude was maintained in the following year's report in October 1968 in which the Committee's faith was placed in the development of Citizens Advice Bureaux (CABx) as a solution to the problem of unmet legal need. However, outside these official circles other developments in the debate over unmet need were already under way. In January 1967 the problems facing the legal profession had been the subject of a conference held by the Society of Labour Lawyers at which a committee had been elected 'to examine the present provision of legal and other advisory services to the community, to consider possible ways of improving such services, and to make recommendations' (Society of Labour Lawyers, 1968:1).

In the same year two other investigations into legal services also took place. The Lord Chancellor's Advisory Committee though sceptical of the concept of law centres was, nevertheless, aware of the criticism directed at the then existing provision of Legal Aid. Accordingly, it asked the Law Society to make a detailed study of the provision of legal advice and assistance (Lord Chancellor's Office, 1967:50). Finally, the Society of Conservative Lawyers in June 1967 elected a committee to prepare its own report on the future shape of legal services (Society of Conservative Lawyers, 1968:5).

First into print with its views was the Law Society in February 1968. This memorandum dealt with what later became known as the £25 scheme under which a solicitor could provide legal advice and assistance (but not litigation) up to the amount specified without prior approval from the Legal Aid authorities. The Law Society also advocated the creation of an Advisory Liaison Service in order to provide an effective link between the private profession and agencies such as CABx and social services departments whose clients are often in need of legal services. A liaison officer, so it appeared from the memorandum, would be able to attend at a CAB, for instance, and to offer simple advice to clients. He could also ascertain the nature of their legal problems and refer clients to an appropriate panel of local solicitors from which clients could choose a solicitor to handle more detailed legal issues. Liaison officers were intended to be a more effective mechanism of directing clients to private practitioners. The Advisory Liaison Scheme was, therefore, the Law Society's answer to the problem of unmet legal need, and in the view of the Society its solution was far preferable to one involving the creation of law centres. According to the Law Society (1968:6, para 21):

the existing advice service, based on the practitioner in his office already accustomed to advising, has proved more beneficial than the method originally contemplated of basing advice on salaried solicitors would have been. They would regard a departure from this as a serious mistake.

The Law Society raised five fundamental objections to the proposed creation and operation of law centres.

(a) It contemplates a radical departure from the concept of legal aid as so far developed in this country and, by introducing a separate and distinct legal service, it would exercise a divisive social influence.

(b) It is based upon notions of indigency and charity constituting a step backwards towards a poor person's procedure.

(c) It eliminates, and would introduce confusion over, the legal aid principle of obligation to contribute, wherever reasonable to expect this.

(d) It would be expensive both in overheads and remuneration of the solicitors involved, unless they were those who were too young or old or incompetent to attain the higher salary levels.

(e) As public money would be involved it would be necessary to set up an organisation to control its application (Law Society, 1968:5 – 6, para 20).

In August 1968 the committee of the Society of Labour Lawyers charged with producing a report on the future of legal services presented its first draft to a weekend conference of lawyers in Oxford.

The draft report welcomed the Law Society's proposed £25 scheme and the Advisory Liaison Scheme, but it thought these did not go far enough. The chief recommendation of the draft report was that local legal centres, staffed by salaried lawyers and modelled on the American neighbourhood law centres, should be established in poverty areas. Nothing less than the introduction of a new public service to operate alongside, and in supplement to, the private profession would suffice to deal adequately with the problem of providing proper legal service to those sections of the public who went short of them. Local legal centres were needed to provide high quality legal service to those parts of our cities where the existing need was greatest. What was needed was centres sited in areas where there were few solicitors. Such centres could develop services in ways that were impracticable or even undesirable for private practitioners. They would be open in the evenings and at weekends. They could undertake education of the public about legal services generally and the uses of the legal system. By promoting public knowledge about legal rights they could begin to overcome the barriers and inhibitions which hampered the existing system. Lawyers in legal centres could develop expertise in the legal problems of the poor (Zander, 1978:66).

These differences in attitude towards law centres between the Society of Labour Lawyers and the Law Society were apparent from the moment the Law Society had published its memorandum early in 1968. In order to discuss these differences the Society of Labour Lawyers invited the Law Society to send a representative to the Oxford conference. That representative was Seton Pollock who in a lengthy address to the conference spoke 'not one sentence that indicated support of any kind for the concept of local legal centres as proposed in the draft report' (Zander, 1978:70). Despite protestations by Pollock (1975:94) that the Law Society was not against a salaried sector within the existing Legal Aid scheme, Zander argued that the truth appeared to be

that the Law Society in 1968 was actively against the idea of salaried solicitors providing legal services out of public funds. Naturally, it was particularly hostile to the suggestion that salaried solicitors should be managed by a new structure in which the Law Society would play only a modest role. But it was also opposed to the idea of state salaried lawyers as such (Zander, 1978:70).

The debate continued with the publication of the Society of Labour Lawyers' *Justice for All* in December 1968, largely unchanged from the draft report discussed at the Oxford conference. In the same month the Society of Conservative Lawyers published *Rough Justice* which, beyond endorsing as a last resort the creation of a few experimental law centres, had very little subsequent influence. In contrast, *Justice for All* was such an imaginative document that the Law Society could not simply ignore its message. After due consideration of that message the Law Society produced in July 1969 its second memorandum in which it made a complete about – turn in its policy. Whereas in the first memorandum the Law Society had opposed state salaried solicitors, it now proposed to employ them itself through an expanded Advisory Liaison Service. The new service was to create permanent advisory centres in certain localities to provide legal advice and assistance. Moreover, it was also

to set up permanent local centres...adapted to the general needs of the district including, if necessary, representation in magistrates' courts and county courts and the conduct of litigation so far as this cannot be absorbed by solicitors' firms (Law Society, 1969:9, para 36).

How is one to explain this change in direction? Zander argued that in any explanation the following two factors were probably involved.

One was that officials at the Law Society had broadly come to accept that the idea of salaried solicitors would not go away and that, properly controlled, it even had

31

some merit as a mechanism for solving some of the problems in the legal services field (Zander, 1978:73). The second factor was that

the Law Society feared that if a Labour Government were to win the then forthcoming General Election, it would be likely to implement the proposals of the Society of Labour Lawyers, and the Law Society would then lose control of this new development in the provision of legal services. If state salaried solicitors were to be established, the Law Society wanted to be in charge (Zander, 1978:73).

In the event, it was the Conservative Party and not Labour that won the 1970 general election. Even so, the Law Society's about – face on law centres was to bear some political fruit. The Lord Chancellor's Advisory Committee had been asked to review the proposals of the Law Society and of the societies of Labour and Conservative lawyers, and in January 1970 it produced a special report, which largely favoured the Law Society. The Committee doubted that the management structure proposed by the Labour Lawyers could effectively shield local legal centres from governmental pressures and, therefore, having conceded the case for the creation of such agencies, it preferred that the centres be run by the Law Society (Report of the Advisory Committee, 1970:7, para 19). The Committee also felt that vesting control of law centres with the Law Society would have the advantage that the administration of an additional kind of legal aid service would fall into the hands of the same institution already responsible for the administration of the Civil Legal Aid scheme. Having received this sign of official approval, the Law Society's proposals to set up and run its own publicly funded local legal centres were incorporated into the Legal Advice and Assistance Act of 1972. The Act introduced both the £25 scheme and Advisory Liaison Officers, while Part II empowered the Law Society to employ salaried solicitors in local legal centres for the purpose of giving legal advice and assistance.

The opportunity to develop a network of law centres, whose operations would be funded by central government and whose day – to – day activities would be controlled by the Law society, was available. Had the Conservative Government decided to follow this legislative path open to them, the subsequent development and history of the law centre movement would have been vastly different. However, just as the Conservative Government of the 1980s decided to ignore the recommendations of the Royal Commission on Legal Services concerning the creation of a publicly funded network of law centres, so the Heath administration failed to make any monies available to set up Part II legal centres. While this lack of funding was initially deplored by the Lord Chancellor's Advisory Committee, by the time the Committee gave its evidence to the Royal Commission on Legal Services in 1977 it made no mention of legal centres to be administered by the Law Society. In effect, the idea of Part II legal centres had fallen into decline in official circles. The major reason for this decline was that innovative developments had taken place elsewhere, which demonstrated the inadequacy of the Law Society's proposals to run its own law centres.

The Creation Of The First British Law Centre

In July 1970, relying on charitable funds, Britain's first law centre opened in North Kensington, London. According to Byles and Morris (1977:55), the move

> to set up law centres in this country undoubtedly represented an attempt by a group of 'concerned' lawyers and others to make the legal system work more efficiently and at the same time more economically in the interests of social justice. In so doing they were clearly influenced by North American experience...

The 'concerned' lawyers were essentially those of the Society of Labour Lawyers, and North Kensington Neighbourhood Law Centre (NLC) was the first physical manifestation of that group's values. Opening amidst a great deal of publicity, the centre was dedicated to providing

> a first – class solicitors' service for the people of the North Kensington community; a service which is easily accessible, not intimidating, to which they can turn for guidance as they would to their family doctor, or as someone who can afford it would turn to his family solicitor (North Kensington NLC, 1971:4).

The idea of opening a British law centre was certainly a novel one. However, the manner in which North Kensington NLC dispensed its services was essentially traditional. The centre adopted an open – door policy since its main goal was to open up access to the law for individuals; a policy that immediately resulted in the centre becoming overburdened with individual cases (Byles and Morris, 1977:30 – 1 and 58). Whereas in America legal services became a feature of the 'War on Poverty' and were intended, at least in part, to provide aggressive legal and community action to ameliorate the position of the poor, in Britain there was no such intention.

> No such goals were adumbrated for centres in this country either in the pages of 'Justice for All', or in the records of discussions which preceded the setting up of the first of such centres – in North Kensington (Byles and Morris, 1977:55).

In fact, *Justice for All* carried only an appendix on the American experience of law centres. The idea of law centres was taken from that experience, but their proposed operation did not incorporate the radical methods and goals espoused by some of the more notable agencies, such as California Rural Legal Assistance. The style of operation proposed for British law centres owed much more to the traditional, one – to – one, solicitors' service than to the group – based, proactive strategies of some American centres. Thus it became clear that in the opinion of the Society of Labour Lawyers (1968:61) what was required was a

new institution...capable of bringing high quality legal services to those parts of our cities where the need for them is greatest, and attracting men of ability to the service of the community.

However, no radical restructuring of the manner in which legal services were to be delivered was envisaged; rather, resources were to be distributed and utilised more efficiently but in the context of a traditional and reactive style of operation. Indeed, the services of law centres were to 'co – exist with and be supplemental to the service provided by the private profession' (Society of Labour Lawyers, 1968:61). Furthermore, Byles and Morris have argued that the pages of *Justice for All*

were filled with words of reassurance aimed at mollifying those private practitioners who feared that the introduction of a salaried service – albeit on such a limited scale – would result in a loss of work. Thus not only were a whole range of issues to be excluded from the caseload of projected law centres, but equally it was explained that their existence would generate new work for the private sector. At that time the American concern with social change was nowhere reflected in new plans for the delivery of legal services in this country (Byles and Morris, 1977:55 – 6).

The Labour Lawyers in their report were concerned to bring social justice within reach of many more ordinary citizens, to develop expertise in the special legal problems of the socially and economically disadvantaged, and to deliver legal services in an informal manner. They were also just as concerned

to retain the personal solicitor – client relationship which is a main strength of the private legal system. Clients would be encouraged to seek out the particular lawyer of their choice within the centre, and the work of the centre should so far as possible be organised so as to enable a continuing personal relationship to be maintained. The English tradition of the 'family solicitor', performing general advisory functions, should be incorporated into the working of the centres: for it is a professional man in such a position of trust who is best placed to assist the individual to deal with his problems, whether or not they are likely to lead to litigation (Society of Labour Lawyers, 1968:39).

The 'family solicitor' was the term employed by North Kensington NLC to describe its own services, and it is clear both from the tone of the material within *Justice for All* and from the style of operation subsequently adopted at Britain's first law centre that the origins of the law centre movement were predominantly traditional and reactive. It was on this early and influential example of reactivity at North Kensington NLC that many other law centres were later modelled.

At the time of North Kensington's creation, however, the advantages of the reactive approach seemed straightforward. Moreover, the work of the proposed law centres certainly seemed to provide a more effective method of securing access to legal services for poor people than the existing Legal Aid system. In effect, law centres, such as North Kensington, were a response to, and a great improvement on, the deficiencies of the Legal Aid scheme and of the geographical maldistribution of private solicitors. Law centres provided easy access to lower – income clients and supplied expertise in relevant legal spheres. They also promoted a greater public awareness of legal rights and they undertook tribunal and emergency work, which the private profession often found to be unprofitable or else was not equipped to handle. New expertise and experience in social welfare law were also developed. Finally, the very creation of law centres pointed to the possibility of providing legal services in imaginative ways, so much so that the idea of Part II legal centres, run by the Law Society, soon came to be viewed as an entirely inadequate response to the problems of supplying legal services to the poor.

Although law centres provided these kinds of services and advantages for their clients, the operation of open – door, reactive centres was not to be without serious difficulties. Thus, the original reactive emphases of the law centre movement and of its first concrete manifestation in North Kensington are important in two main ways. First, they set a style of operation that many subsequent law centres were to adopt and, second, the reactive orientation was chiefly responsible for causing many of the serious difficulties that have characterized the work of the majority of British law centres.

North Kensington: An Initial And Influential Example Of Reactivity

In its second annual report North Kensington Law Centre reported that it had

> opened with a full – time staff of three, a number which was totally inadequate to cope with the flood of cases which poured in. We have gradually expanded to the present complement of eight; but in spite of this, and in spite of the invaluable help of many volunteers, legal and non – legal, the pressure of work has never diminished. Members of staff work well beyond their contract hours, frequently having to attend the Centre at weekends to catch up with work (North Kensington NLC, 1972:3).

As a consequence of this overload, also coupled with financial difficulties, the centre was unable 'to look beyond the immediate problems and crises of the clients. The Centre has tended to operate as a normal solicitor's office, giving advice and trying to find

remedies to the problems of individuals on a case by case basis...'
(North Kensington NLC, 1972:3).

The centre's review of its first ten years of operation noted that during 'the first three years, some 1,100 to 1,300 files were opened per year. A gradual shift of resources away from casework brought this total down to some 700 – 800 from 1975 on' (North Kensington NLC, 1980:7). While it is true that North Kensington Law Centre has over the years undertaken proportionately more project and groupwork (though remaining a predominantly open – door reactive centre), the shift in resources was not a gradual one. On the contrary, it was concluded relatively swiftly and was largely due to matters outside the control of the centre. The evidence for this is as follows, and it highlights how difficult it is for reactive law centres to implement specific policies of their own design significantly to alter the reactive approach.

During the first seven months of operation from its opening in July 1970 the centre handled a total of 629 cases, 191 of which (30.3%) were housing cases (North Kensington NLC, 1971:5). During the first 18 months 2,000 cases were opened of which 33% involved housing matters (North Kensington NLC, 1972:1). Throughout the whole of 1972 the centre reported that 'the pressure on the staff...has steadily increased as is reflected by the increasing number of visits by clients to the law centre. The great majority of cases are the same as in previous years' (North Kensington NLC, 1973:6). In 1973, 1,314 cases were opened and of these 40% comprised housing matters (North Kensington NLC, 1974:3). No figures were available separately for the year 1974 but in the period January to December 1975 the centre opened a total of 796 files, of which 162 (21%) were housing cases (North Kensington NLC, 1975:22).

There is no 'gradual shift' at all. Throughout the latter half of 1970, the whole of 1971, 1972 and 1973 individual case levels remained very high and staff reported that they were overworked and inundated with cases. The decrease in individual cases presumably began during 1974 and was reflected in the figures available for the year 1975. The large fall in case levels from approximately 1,200 to 1,300 per annum upto and including 1973 to approximately 800 per annum in 1975 was not by any means wholly attributable to any decision by the law centre staff to reduce the level of individual casework and to pursue more proactive endeavours. On the contrary, the major part of the fall in individual cases between 1973 and 1975 can be accounted for (and is reflected also in reports of other law centres at this period) in terms of changes in both the legal and local community environment in which the centre operated. Indeed, North Kensington Law Centre (1975:22) itself has acknowledged this fact.

> Much of the overall reduction in our caseload is attributable to three main factors:
> 1. The improvement in the situation of furnished tenants following the 1974 Rent Act

2. The effect of the Duty Solicitor Scheme at Marylebone Magistrates Court.
3. The number of large 'representative' actions where one case may include 100 tenants.

North Kensington Law Centre's operational existence has been characterized largely by the servicing of individual cases, and its attempts to adopt a more proactive approach have been slow in progressing, and occasionally have failed altogether (North Kensington NLC, 1980:10 – 12). For instance, the intention to employ a community worker met with no success at all during the centre's first three years of operation. As Byles and Morris (1977:18) reported:

> initially the pressure of individual casework was felt to make it necessary to concentrate on the appointment of legal staff (and secretaries to service them), and later, when applications were made to various charitable organisations for the funding of a community worker, these were unsuccessful. Had the Management Committee been unanimous in supporting such a move earlier on, it is possible that despite these difficulties an appointment would have been pushed through, but even when, at a later date, funds were forthcoming, and the proposal was put before the committee, some of the more senior legal members were wary of the implications of such an appointment...and it was decided that the appointment of a full – time receptionist would make a more significant contribution to the work of the Centre.

In an 18 year review of the operation of the centre in 1988, the argument was put forward that: 'Project and educational work has only gradually become a legitimate function of a law centre' (Chakraborty et al, 1988:20).

Byles and Morris identified three models of law centre operation; the first, model 'A', approximating to a reactive style of work. Model 'A' consisted of a salaried legal service that extended to 'the poor community a traditional service similar in structure to that provided to middle – class clients by private practitioners (Byles and Morris, 1977:57). From their research at North Kensington Law Centre these authors concluded that the agency

> was set up in accordance with Model 'A' and the service provided has remained almost exclusively upon the adoption of a professional posture vis – a – vis individual clients. Although professional advice has readily been made available to community groups and organisations, there has been a reluctance to become at all closely involved in what may be interpreted (very widely) as 'political' activities, and even law reform and community education have been largely eschewed (Byles and Morris, 1977:57).

This description of the origins and early development of North Kensington NLC outlines the various factors that influenced both the initial and continuing reactive emphases within the centre. As I indicated towards the end of Chapter Two, the factors influencing levels of reactivity fall into four main categories; namely, the original organization of the agency, modifications to that organization as achieved by staff and clientele, levels of funding, and the nature of 'external ' constraints. North Kensington NLC was dedicated to providing a first – class, open – door solicitor's service. It was assumed that the centre would be handling cases on an individual basis and that the solicitor – client, relationship would be structured along relatively traditional lines[1]. As case levels grew so did the number of staff, who also attempted to conduct some 'representative' work with groups of tenants. For the most part, however, a substantial period of the history of the centre was one of servicing individual cases on a one – to – one basis. Indeed, the centre has struggled to achieve even this goal as it would prefer, given its insufficient resources. Some changes in the legal environment, such as the creation of a duty solicitors' scheme and the passing of the Rent Act 1974, enabled the centre to reduce its levels of individual cases in some areas. However, other 'external' factors, such as a number of influential figures on the centre's management committee, were not conducive to the development of a greater emphasis on group and community work. These factors taken as a whole not only moulded the pattern of reactivity at the centre, but also prevented it from developing any significant emphasis on a participatory and more proactive ethos.

The reactive origins and style of North Kensington NLC recurred elsewhere in the law centre movement. Indeed, the Urban Community Law Centre (1978a:1), which is to be the subject of a detailed case – study in Chapter Four, explicitly acknowledged that it 'was based on the experience of the very first law centre, North Kensington Law Centre, from which...[its] first solicitors came'. In addition to the achievements of the reactive law centres, there were also considerable problems of operation, which staff tried to overcome. These problems and the attempts to solve them will be the focus of the next chapter. However, although the majority of law centres that came into existence after North Kensington were largely reactive in their emphases, a few proactive law centres were setting an entirely different example of delivering legal services to the poor.

Towards Proactive Alternatives

Although *Justice for All* carried an appendix on the proactive goals of the American Legal Services Program – community education, law reform, community action, and the participation of the poor – these themes were not reflected strongly in the work of North Kensington nor of most other UK law centres. However, within what was a predominantly reactive approach to the delivery of legal services, there were some examples of proactive law centres.

In 1971 the Northern Neighbourhood Law Centre began its work as did what was later formally to become Brent Law Centre. In 1972 the Adamsdown centre, which had always been sympathetic towards proactive activities, started its work, and in 1973 Newham Rights Centre opened. In their separate ways the activities of these centres became known to the law centre movement, which was itself simultaneously beginning to realize many of the difficulties associated with the reactive approach. By 1974 the Law Centres' Working Group had formed to represent the interests of the movement and to act as a forum in which new ideas to overcome such difficulties could be aired. In the same year the Working Group (subsequently renamed the Law Centres' Federation) published *Towards Equal Justice*, which argued that law centres should place greater emphasis on community education and action. The document stated that all law centres

> have come to recognise that, while casework for individual members of a community in the traditional style of legal profession is of great help to those individual clients, if lawyers, or, at least, groups of lawyers, are to use their skills to the full to help those communities in their efforts to end their 'deprivation' they will have to change their manner of working in a number of ways (Law Centres' Federation, 1974:1, para 1.1).

Towards Equal Justice outlined the manner in which those ways of working should be changed. In this sense, the document was a policy statement about the manner in which law centres might achieve a more proactive approach; it was not an empirical account of the then actual operations of law centres, nor did it reflect the serious problems many reactive law centres were to encounter in their attempts to become significantly more proactive. Nevertheless, the ideals or goals embodied in *Towards Equal Justice* were clearly set out. Thus, it was ·deemed

> the duty of those who seek to provide legal services in poor and working class communities to concentrate their resources on helping people of those communities to create organisations capable of helping their members with their collective difficulties. Further, once these organisations exist, it is the duty of lawyers to use their skills in helping the organisations in their relations with outsiders. Not only is this a service which the established legal profession has failed to provide, and for financial and ideological reasons is incapable of providing, but it is also a means whereby scarce resources of qualified legal manpower can be put to the best use on behalf of the greatest number of people (Law Centres' Federation, 1974:7 – 8, para 2.10).

The document stressed the need for and effectiveness of organizing working – class people into community groups, and it stated too that law centres should pursue a wider range of tactics than simply that of litigation. Moreover, it asserted that a major aim of law centres 'must be to reduce the need for casework' (Law Centres' Federation, 1974:11, para 3.3). Furthermore, it argued that through advising and helping local groups and through combating ignorance of the law, law centres could 'hope not only to make people aware of their existing rights but also to give them the knowledge and confidence to enforce them' (Law Centres' Federation, 1974:13, para 3.7).

While individual proactive law centres produced their own detailed versions of such goals – as I shall show in Chapter Five – the principles set out in *Towards Equal Justice* are clearly vital components in any proactive approach. Indeed, although the language used in the document differs in many respects from the conceptual terms I have been employing, nevertheless *Towards Equal Justice* was essentially a description of proactivity. Indeed, the quotations taken from it and reproduced above highlight the need for law centres to become involved in party upgrading; to share knowledge with clients and to encourage the development of client competences by employing people – working skills; and to pursue legal and non – legal strategies in attempts to realize the rights of citizenship. Also subsumed under the concerns of *Towards Equal Justice* are the issues of informed consent, the nature of the lawyer – client relationship, and consumer control. All of these issues will be the subject of Chapter Five in which I shall describe the work of the proactive law centres and evaluate their achievements and failures. Before that, however, I propose to conduct a similar exercise in relation to Britain's reactive law centres.

Notes

1. North Kensington Law Centre, *The First Ten Years* (1980:7) reported that the original proposals for the centre appeared 'to assume that the centre would be doing only casework, that its work would be structured primarily by the solicitor/client relationship. The first solicitor, who remained the senior solicitor for over seven years, conceived of the centre as offering a universal casework service to all low – income residents in its catchment area'.

4 The weight of reactivity: the caseload deluge

This chapter will cover the period from 1973 – 4, the time of the creation of several law centres following the opening of Britain's first such agency at the start of the decade, to 1979, the year by which the formative development of the law centre movement was completed and in which also the Royal Commission on Legal Services reported. This period represented the steady growth of the law centre movement in which both its achievements and prevailing difficulties became evident. I shall concentrate on the activities of reactive law centres and describe how many of these centres tried to overcome the operational problems associated with a predominantly reactive approach. I shall also be using some data gathered in the period 1975 to 1978 when I was conducting empirical research on the Urban Community Law Centre (UCLC), a predominantly reactive agency. In Chapter Six I shall be covering the period from 1980 to the present day, showing how law centres are coping with contemporary problems.

Coping With Caseloads

One of the major effects of a predominantly reactive, open – door approach to the delivery of legal services is the high level of individual cases generated. High caseloads have constituted a major difficulty in the operation of reactive law centres from their inception, and there are numerous examples that could be cited. Among them is the work of Balham Neighbourhood Law Centre (BNLC), which reported in 1974 that it was 'anxious that the staff should not be overwhelmed by casework in the first few months. For this reason, there will not be much publicity about opening' (BNLC, 1973 – 4:4). Balham Law Centre was obviously aware that other law centres had been inundated with cases upon opening, and it hoped to avoid a similar fate by, so to speak, keeping quiet about its own opening. However, such hopes were to prove ill – founded for in the following year the centre stated that it was

> one of many agencies that is in danger of being swamped by housing casework. The staff agreed unanimously that it must attempt to educate the public about the waste of time and money involved in taking case after case, instead of trying to find a real solution to the housing situation. A start was made by the survey of empty property...' (BNLC, 1974 – 5:5).

To poor people in the centre's catchment area, an opportunity to enjoy professional services free of charge did not appear to be a waste of time as far as they were concerned. Consequently, individual demand for the law centre's services remained high. Indeed, the property survey was carried out in the context of continuing pressure on staff from large caseloads, which eventually forced the centre to increase the number of cases it referred to local private solicitors and to enforce more rigorously its policy governing the acceptance of cases. These changes, made between April 1975 and March 1976, were a direct response to the fact that the centre

> could only just cope with the number of people needing legal advice and assistance. Workers began this year with established caseloads, and previous clients returning for second and subsequent interviews for ongoing actions. The number of new clients coming to the centre is 20% higher than last year (BNLC, 1975 – 6:3).

One way in which the staff felt they could reduce this number was to make 'people more independent...to encourage them to act for themselves at tribunals and in some court cases' (BNLC, 1975 – 6:5). At the same time the centre also 'continued to take every opportunity that has presented itself to help groups of tenants to solve their own problems' (BNLC, 1976 – 7:4); and it did in fact enjoy some moderate success in pursuing this aim. Another of its aims was to educate local residents in the law and its operation, but while aware of the advantages of such an approach the centre reported that it had 'not done so much in this area as we would like because of the greater immediacy of the needs of individual cases' (BNLC, 1976 – 7:7). The position was such that the pressure of 'work and the desire to place greater resources in legal education led the staff and management committee after very lengthy discussions and with some regret to decide to close two more afternoons a week from June 1977' (BNLC, 1976 – 7:8). The next year did see some increase in the amount of educational work handled by the centre, and the numbers of new cases and inquiries did fall somewhat. However, this fall was mainly because the Centre unfortunately had to be closed for two months at the beginning of the year to enable emergency building work to be undertaken. The amount of further action taken by the Centre was also reduced because of the lack of one permanent solicitor for parts of the year, and because of a change in emphasis in the Centre towards helping people to help themselves more, both through giving more thorough advice on reception rather than taking on cases, and through our outside education programme (BNLC, 1977 – 8:2).

Balham Law Centre clearly tried to implement a number of strategies designed not only to reduce individual casework but also to allow the centre to become somewhat more proactive and, thus, to place greater emphasis on developing client competence by involving them actively in seeking solutions to their problems. However, progress towards such a goal in the period 1973 to 1978 was slow. Indeed, such progress that was made in reducing caseloads was mainly the result of the centre's enforced closure and the loss of a solicitor rather than the outcome of explicit planning by the staff. On its own admission Balham was primarily a casework service that occasionally took up broader issues arising out of its individual cases. However, only a small proportion of staff time was expended on these broader issues (BNLC, 1977 – 8:1).

A similar history of a law centre firmly entrenched within a predominantly reactive style comes from Hackney Law Centre, an agency linked directly with a Citizens Advice Bureau, which reported that its staff continued

to discuss the balance between the casework and the other work of the centre. The demands, particularly from individuals, upon all sections of the centre makes this difficult, as...the volume of work dealt with by the centre is considerable. There is a danger of the workers being swamped by casework so that there is no opportunity to stand back and look at the broader issues of the centre's work and direction (Annual Report of Hackney Advice Bureau and Law Centre, 1976 – 7:7).

The following year (1977 – 8) gave no respite from the flow of cases and in order to cope with its workload the Citizens Advice Bureau had to reduce its opening hours from August 1977. Despite this attempt to reduce the number of clients referred to the law centre by the CAB, the

continued pressure of cases has made it difficult for the Centre to expand its involvement as far as it hoped with local groups and to take part in activities of a more educational nature or do more general research into the needs of the area (Annual Report of Hackney Advice Bureau and Law Centre, 1977 – 8:11).

Handsworth Law Centre (HLC) stated that it was looking forward to a period of growth in its project work and in community education. Despite a high staff turnover during 1978 – 9 the centre was able to initiate a small number of project groups within the agency whose brief it was to identify wider issues arising out of individual casework.

Perhaps because housing disrepair is such a big issue for council tenants and so easily definable in both casework and campaigning terms for HLC, this particular project group has been amongst the most successful. There is one caveat, however, that needs to be voiced. The heavy volume of casework has tended to detract from the campaigning side of the project. The following year must see this imbalance put right, since there is little evidence to support the view that individual complaints, no matter how numerous, effect any general improvement in the Housing Department's approach to this problem (Handsworth Law Centre, 1978 – 9:11).

Paddington Law Centre, also linked to a CAB, experienced difficulties with high caseloads from the time it first opened in 1973. In its second year of operation, the centre reported that:

Following a couple of relatively short periods when the staff became so overladen with work that they could only accept referrals which were emergencies, we decided, after much heart – searching, that as from the end of the year under review, the catchment area of the Law Centre would have to be restricted and the greater part of W.2 postal district had to be abandoned (Paddington Neighbourhood Advice Bureau and Law Centre, 1975:11).

In 1975, the centre's third year of existence, the continuing high caseloads had further consequences. The centre noted that

the decline in the number of referrals from Tenants and Residents groups – the basic community organisation in the area – is worrying and does reflect both the shortage of money and the pressure on our staff which has prevented them from developing more fully the relationship with local community organisations (Paddington Neighbourhood Advice Bureau and Law Centre, 1976:5).

The pressure and the relative failure to upgrade the capacity and competence of local groups continued, so much so that in 1976 the centre did not accept new clients for a three month period. This allowed staff 'substantially to catch up on the back – log' of cases (Paddington Advice and Law Centre, 1976 – 8:3). In order to improve matters both the law centre and the CAB staff decided to introduce a more 'rational working system' that would allow more resources to be devoted to working with groups. The centre stated:

This far – reaching re – distribution of resources can only be implemented gradually, and indeed, as this report is written, their re – direction is not fully operative (Paddington Advice and Law Centre, 1976 – 8:6).

In 1975 Islington Law Centre reported that:

Certainly we are trying to reduce our own workload; we are now rejecting small accident and consumer claims. But, whatever we do to reduce the load of appointments or eliminate certain types of cases, the pressure goes on (Islington Community Law Centre, 1975:2).

A similar story emerged at Small Heath Law Centre at which, within three months of opening at the beginning of 1977,

the pressure of work meant that a lot of work for existing clients was falling behind and it was therefore decided that it was necessary to vary the opening hours to allow the staff more time to actually do the work they were taking on (Small Heath Community Law Centre, 1976 – 7:24).

The staff had planned to devote resources to more proactive projects and had placed certain restrictions on the acceptance of individual cases even before the centre had opened. Even so, they found that

when the Centre opened with what amounted to six caseworkers and a community worker, it was immediately swamped with cases, so much so that the staff functioned effectively as seven caseworkers. One result of this was that individual members of staff were concentrating on their own areas of work to the exclusion of other areas; this resulted in isolation, which impaired the efficiency of the Centre and meant there was no communication between interrelated areas of work (Small Heath Community Law Centre, 1977 – 8:4).

Given this situation the staff tried to improve the imbalance between individual casework and more proactive activities. Thus, opening hours were changed; more cases were referred to other agencies; and the staff were restructured into various units in an attempt to create the time and flexibility required to pursue proactive work. At the end of June 1978 there had been an 'increase in group work and issue work (although not balanced with a corresponding decrease in individual casework)', made possible by the appointment of an extra general worker allocated to the community unit (Small Heath Community Law Centre, 1977 – 8:4). While restructuring the staff into units was felt to have allowed the centre to cope more effectively with community demands, 'the strain of an increasing amount of individual casework is still being felt' (Small Heath Community Law Centre, 1977 – 8:5). That strain was still there in 1979 when further decisions were taken regarding priorities for the acceptance of cases. The structure of the centre's units also underwent some slight alterations. A quota system was introduced for members of staff handling individual cases, limiting the number that any staff member could take on at one time. In order to compensate for what amounted to a reduction in the overall level of 'active' individual cases, more detailed advice was given to clients and even more use was made of referrals to other agencies. All of these changes were made in response to the fact that 'the staff were becoming swamped by the amount of work coming through the door and this meant that there was a real risk of deterioration in the standard of work carried out for individual clients' (Small Heath Community Law Centre, 1978 – 9:4).

The final brief example comes from Vauxhall Law Centre, which stated in its second annual report that the number of cases coming to the agency had 'apparently more than doubled, and this despite the fact that for about three months we were taking on no new cases at all because of the pressure of work' (Vauxhall Community Law Centre, 1974 – 5:1). Two years later Vauxhall reported that it was trying 'to do less individual casework. We continued to try to help people where possible, but we had found that by doing so many individual cases we were unable to take stock of what we were doing and we were failing to deal with broader issues' (Vauxhall Community Law Centre, 1976 – 7:2).

The problems encountered by the law centres I have briefly described stemmed from their predominantly reactive emphases. The main issues associated with the reactive orientation, which have emerged so far, are high caseloads, unacceptable pressures and workloads on law centre staff, a tendency towards a deterioration in the quality of service for clients, and the emergence of operational difficulties in attempts to shift the emphasis from a heavily reactive one to a more proactive style. Attempts to implement such a shift have included the following: restricting opening hours and size of catchment area; resetting priorities for acceptance and rejection of cases; evolving more efficient referral systems; employing more part – time volunteer lawyers and non – lawyers; increasing the number of advice – only cases; preparing self – help leaflets; and, finally, rationalizing the number and type of cases referred to the law centre by conducting 'educational' work with the referring agencies.

In the remainder of the chapter I shall focus in detail on the work of the Urban Community Law Centre (UCLC) in order to explain more fully the attitudes of the staff that lay behind attempts to reduce individual caseloads and to become more proactive. The analysis of UCLC will also allow me to address various conceptual issues, such as the nature of the lawyer – client relationship, informed consent, client competence, etc., and to investigate to what extent these concepts are realized within the context of a reactive law centre. Just as there were a number of common issues running through the examples already provided of reactive law centres, the conceptual themes, which I will explore through an analysis of the work of UCLC, similarly apply to the operational experiences of many other reactive law centres in the UK. In this sense, UCLC is a kind of metaphor for the achievements and problems associated with reactive law centres.

The Origins Of UCLC

The Urban Community Law Centre, opened in 1973 and funded by the local authority, was largely based on the model of North Kensington Law Centre. During discussions in 1972 about the need for a law centre in the locality, two divergent views emerged. On the one hand, there were some local community groups that favoured the idea that the law centre should act as a resource for such neighbourhood groups and for other advice – giving agencies. On the other hand, some local authority councillors supported the view that the law centre should become an alternative solicitor's office offering a free casework service to the poor of the borough. The subsequent management committee of UCLC with a membership drawn from the council, the Law Society, local advice agencies, and community groups, reflected these two views. Indeed, both a reactive and a proactive emphasis were incorporated into the centre's constitution, which required the centre to fulfil three functions.

First, UCLC was to provide free legal advice and assistance to poor people resident in the borough. Second, it was to undertake research into the impact of the law on the local community. Third, the centre was mandated to develop educational work with local people to provide them with information about the law and its operation. While the second and third elements of the centre's constitution may be seen as proactive undertakings with an obvious 'outreach' capacity, the first constitutional requirement was interpreted by the local council to mean that UCLC would become an open – door law centre with high public visibility and access. There was little discussion about the danger that an over – emphasis on servicing individual cases might prevent the law centre from fulfilling its other constitutional duties. Thus, from the very beginning of UCLC's work, it was the first constitutional requirement that dominated its operations (UCLC, 1978a:2). It was never made clear in the planning for the centre how UCLC was to combine effectively the reactive and proactive emphases written into its constitution.

One important reason why this issue was not explored at UCLC was that the

> group proposing the law centre had only one model in Britain to look at, North Kensington Law Centre, which was dealing with an enormous amount of criminal work. Although this was easily seen as endless individual casework, it could also be seen as group or issue work in its widest sense, since one of the key problems was the breakdown in relations between police and young blacks in the area. North Kensington came into existence because of support from active community groups, then acted at first as though access to the law was the key problem, and had a shop – front and an open door. This was partly dictated by the need for a large legal aid

income for the centre to survive, but the result of this was that it was a model which did not make clear the difficulties of different approaches to law centre work (UCLC, 1978b:2a).

In summary, therefore, the position at UCLC was that:

These differences in approach were not spelt out... and were obscured by the functions given to the law centre in its constitution, which include individual casework, work with groups, and educational and research work, but the underlying conflict remained, and has been one of the crucial problems for the law centre, in that the question of priorities and different working methods has been constantly discussed for the past five years and still remains a central question as we attempt to find the most effective and worthwhile way of providing legal services...(UCLC, 1977 – 8:2).

The following account describes how the UCLC staff attempted to cope with the problems of high caseloads and the question of adopting a different style of operation.

Work With Individuals: Setting Priorities For Case Intake And Referral

Mandated to provide legal advice and assistance to poor persons within the borough on all legal matters – save those such as conveyancing, probate, matrimonial, and personal injury cases, which were excluded under the terms of the centre's constitution – UCLC was immediately given a heavy burden. At the very least, the centre offered advice to almost every person that called at the reception area. Clients who could not afford to hire a private solicitor and who had problems that required more detailed attention were taken on by the centre as active cases. Mindful of the advantages of a free service in terms of its attractiveness to clients, UCLC adopted a liberal attitude towards Legal Aid financial eligibility criteria, avoiding where possible the systematic and rigorous means – testing of its clientele. Where for any reason the centre had not felt able to act for some individuals, these people have been referred to local solicitors or to other appropriate agencies. Indeed, the referral or brokerage function of the centre has grown steadily over the years[1], but in the period of my research UCLC had no way of knowing how many of its referred clients actually kept the appointments made for them at these other agencies or private solicitors' offices[2]. Despite some evidence from a legal advice agency in Sheffield[2], which suggested that a high percentage of recommended referrals do take place, UCLC itself had no clear idea about the effectiveness or the quality of this aspect of its work.

The increase in the number of clients over the years who have been referred elsewhere was in part a consequence of the high individual caseloads with which the centre   had to cope from the outset. Far more people came to the centre – which then had its door open for five and a half days and two evenings a week – than could possibly be helped by four solicitors, even when the solicitors were working till late at night and at the weekends. It was difficult for the centre as a whole to remain aware of its community and be responsive to it: what it was responding to was the pressure of people coming through the door. Those who lived too far away or who needed a different kind of legal service were as badly served as ever, except for the very energetic work being done by the community workers, including work with tenants' associations, in schools, running courses on rights and publishing leaflets and booklets. Effective as this work was, it was limited by the inaccessibility of the solicitors, whose casework made it impossible for them to be more than marginally involved in the rest of the work of the centre (UCLC, 1977 – 8:2).

Another consequence of high caseloads was that UCLC began to restrict the kinds of legal issues where it was prepared to act. The original constitutional restrictions were widened in 1974 in an attempt to reduce case numbers. Thus, UCLC stopped handling accident cases and adult criminal work, and it reduced the number of housing cases by referring them to private solicitors when clients were eligible for Legal Aid. In the same year the centre also excluded defamation cases, neighbour disputes, traffic offences, and nearly all consumer work. In 1976 it ceased to represent clients before the Rent Tribunal and Rent Officer.

I am not suggesting that UCLC either could or should have operated a comprehensive legal service. Rather, I am highlighting how its range of services was narrowed as a direct response to the pressures of high caseloads. There is no doubt that the centre's focus on housing, juvenile crime, employment issues, and family and welfare matters was an appropriate one[3]. However, even if UCLC was not comprehensive in its legal coverage, it was nevertheless expected to offer its services throughout the whole borough[4]. In practice, the majority of its clients lived within a short travelling distance of the centre. It attracted relatively few clients from the borough's outlying areas. UCLC staff were aware of this fact but could do little to rectify it. With such pressure on the centre's resources, they were unable to spread its services more evenly throughout the borough by working, for instance, with community groups. Moreover, they were wary of advertising the centre's services and open – door policy in outlying areas for fear of increasing the caseload burden. While UCLC drew its clientele disproportionately from the immediately surrounding locality, there was no doubting its ability to attract large numbers of clients[5]. In fact, this approachability of the centre was a factor in encouraging the use of its services by those who would not normally have gone to a private solicitor. A measure of its approachability was the adoption of a shop – front image for the law centre and its location along a main shopping street. A measure of its success – but which perversely brought its own serious difficulties – was the very high number of cases and individuals attracted to the centre.

The Centre's Research And Training Activities

During the period of my study at UCLC the staple research activity undertaken by the centre was the collection of basic statistics for inclusion in annual reports. These statistics included the number and type of cases handled, the source of referrals to the centre and the destination of those referred by the centre, and the number of advice – only cases. There was very little else by way of systematic research. Given the pressure on resources from high caseloads this was hardly surprising. Moreover, there is one sense in which a reactive law centre like UCLC is not as dependent on community – based research as a proactive centre. At a proactive law centre community – based research of one kind or another is required in order to uncover those issues that are of common importance to various people and groups in the locality. Moreover, some form of data gathering exercise is also required if the strategies adopted by local groups are successfully to address those issues. However, at a reactive law centre most clients receive individualized advice and assistance and data gathering tends to relate to particular individual circumstances – the wider picture is not usually explored. It is only when staff at a reactive law centre wish to uncover underlying patterns among individual cases, to understand their wider social origins, and to explore collective solutions that they begin to appreciate the value of systematic community – based research.

UCLC's training initiatives tell a more successful story. Although in – service training sessions for the centre's staff were discontinued in 1974 due to the pressure of cases, they were reinstated on a weekly basis in 1977. Generally, staff members felt the sessions to have been valuable, especially for those preparing papers for presentation. Training was seen as a way of equipping staff with the skills to cope with high caseloads, in particular for non – legal staff. As a consequence of the heavy caseloads the non – lawyers at UCLC had to take on an increasing responsibility for the conduct of their own individual cases, while those staff manning the reception desks needed to give more detailed advice to clients. In short, as the non – lawyers lost their specific titles as receptionists or secretaries and became known as general workers, so the need for them to develop greater expertise became apparent, especially in advice – giving and in legal procedures. The training sessions were thus intended to enhance the competences of general workers and to ensure that they would need to seek advice and assistance far less from the centre's lawyers, thereby easing the burden on the lawyers and providing for a more efficient service in general. It was difficult to judge how successful in – service training was in these respects. Sessions were thought to have been worthwhile, and the prepared papers on points of law and procedure were useful future reference materials. But it was not possible to measure whether, in fact, general workers did consult lawyers less frequently as a result of training. There were, however, many comments from general workers suggesting that the centre's lawyers remained under heavy caseload pressures, and that this often meant they were too busy to respond to requests from general workers for legal advice and information. Finally, nearly everyone at the centre agreed that the prime beneficiaries of in – service training were not the general workers but the lawyers who were the ones usually preparing and presenting specialist papers.

In later years, the centre began to assist in the training of personnel at other advice – giving agencies in the borough not only to improve the quality of service provided by those agencies, but also in the hope that effective advice at that stage might lessen the number of subsequent referrals to the law centre itself[6].

The Centre And Community Education

The community educational requirement of the centre's constitution may be said to be preventive in its impact in two ways. First, community education tries to make individuals and groups more aware of their rights, which in turn may lead to the avoidance of common problems engendered through ignorance of the law. Second, it encourages self – help solutions to those problems that cannot be avoided. Moreover, the preventive aspect not only potentially applies to clients but also to the centre itself, which would expect to handle fewer enquiries if citizens were themselves better equipped to handle their own problems. Unfortunately, during the period of my study, the fulfilment of these preventive goals was hampered by the relatively low level of resources that the centre was able to devote to its educational and community work activities.

While the centre's community worker believed that a certain amount of individual casework sensitized her to the larger problems of the locality, she felt that her ability to devote her time to community work was severely inhibited by her high caseload and by her need to service these individual cases first. She argued that high caseloads were preventing all the staff, and not just herself, from conducting a larger amount of educational and community work.

UCLC's educational work focused primarily on a small number of local secondary schools where fourth and fifth formers attended a variety of inputs given by the law centre's staff. Topics included the rights of juveniles at arrest and in court, how to claim welfare benefits, and what to do about unfair dismissal. Interesting and novel approaches were employed such as the use of tape and slide shows, lectures and discussions, distribution of leaflets and work – cards, role – playing in a mock – up of a juvenile court, and using video facilities. In contrast, the centre's educational activities with local tenants' associations lacked the coherence of UCLC's work in schools. Typically, the centre responded to ad hoc requests from tenants' associations for information. In more recent years the centre has tried to improve this state of affairs by operating as more of a legal resource for a variety of local agencies and associations. While still being a predominantly open – door reactive agency (although the door is now closed two days during the week), UCLC undertakes what it describes as a 'considerable' amount of legal resource work. This involves the centre giving advice to a range of local groups including CABx, neighbourhood advice centres, housing aid centres, tenants' associations, community centres, and women's and immigrants' groups (UCLC, 1986 – 7:13, and UCLC, 1987 – 8:2). Even as the centre has enjoyed some long overdue success in adopting a somewhat more proactive approach through its legal resource work, UCLC still has to cope with the problem of more people coming to the centre for help than it has the resources with which to deal (UCLC, 1987 – 8:2). The problem of managing high individual case levels with insufficient resources, a dilemma which faced the centre from the very outset, still presents difficulties for the centre's staff today.

Coping With The 'Flood' Of Cases

High caseloads have periodically caused UCLC staff to redraw the centre's priorities and to reflect critically upon its operational philosophy. One such period of reflection took place in November 1976 when a special staff meeting was called to discuss ways in which individual caseloads might be reduced and greater resources thereby channelled towards a more proactive orientation. A brief description of UCLC's chronic caseload problem will provide a greater understanding of why the staff felt such a meeting was necessary.

From the first day that UCLC opened its doors to the public it was inundated with clients, so that each of the solicitors was very soon carrying a caseload of upward of one hundred cases. Excluding certain types of cases did little to stem public demand for the centre's services. Large numbers of clients continued to call at the centre and to telephone for advice[7]. Such pressure led to some of the staff referring to themselves as being 'shell – shocked', and they felt that the time spent servicing individual cases was preventing them from undertaking more group and project work.

This is not a matter of the number of staff, but rather is the result of the way we have worked. In presenting ourselves as yet another advice agency as well as a law centre, we have depended on finding out the needs of the community too much by waiting to see what problems the people came into the centre with. *This has been at the expense of supporting the much wider community network and making resources available to take up the larger group cases and issues which come through it* (UCLC, 1977 – 8:4, Italics added).

Staff were concerned that some planned projects had not got off the ground because the lawyers had been too busy to help launch them. Equally, there was concern that the community work aspects of the centre's role were being undermined by the overwhelming need to service individual cases.

...the two community workers always had more to do than time to do it in, so that on the whole their activity was limited to the areas of the law centre's existing casework – housing and juveniles – and much that they started was not followed up or completed.

A combination of factors – the pressure of casework, the political pressure from the Local Authority, a general merging of the original casework, community work, reception, servicing distinctions amongst staff, etc. – led to the elimination of the community workers' nominated posts, but the work they had been doing was not replaced by a corresponding increase in group and community involvement among the workers as a whole...(UCLC, 1978a:3).

As well as the general disappointment that not more community work was being pursued, there was also an increasing sense of frustration among the law centre staff. Not only did they recognize that case levels were too high, but also they felt that

doing a high level of casework over a long period of time could lead to disillusionment with the long – term effect of the work and dissatisfaction, which could be alleviated so long as the centre's work would include work on projects within the areas of priority covered by the law centre (UCLC, 1976:1).

High levels of casework and the associated pressure on staff led to worker dissatisfaction and also prevented them from

having any opportunity to examine the work done to see what issues of general importance emerge, and what alternative methods of working would be more effective in reaching residents with legal problems or lack of awareness of rights. This kind of pressure would lead to failure to carry out the aims of the constitution of the law centre as well as lowering the job satisfaction of the worker (UCLC, 1976:1).

The answer to the debilitating effects of high caseloads was seen in terms of increasing the level of project work – variously referred to as educational, group, or community work. A study by Katz in Chicago of lawyers employed in a law centre programme demonstrated the personal and professional needs of lawyers to be

53

involved in project work. He found that for lawyers employed to help the poor the project was
a combined personal and collective experiment. In it, the member designs a short range career to extending the organisation's boundaries, elaborate its structure, or increase the resourcefulness of its membership. From the member's standpoint, the 'experimental' nature of the project means *activities will not be routine*. One's abilities to act or understand will be tested in a new way. From the standpoint of the organisation, projects address the capacity to act collectively. They are attempts to develop the character of the organisation (Katz, 1976:199, Italics added).

The November 1976 staff meeting was just such an attempt to find ways of doing more project work; to develop the law centre's organizational capacities; and to provide greater job satisfaction for staff who were servicing large numbers of individual cases in what could be described as a relatively routine fashion. High caseloads, therefore, led not only to staff dissatisfaction, but also to most cases being subject to routine servicing, which in itself contributed to further disenchantment among the centre's personnel. I shall be returning shortly to the issue of routine case processing when I consider the work of UCLC in connection with the realization of citizenship rights. First, however, I shall cover UCLC's attempts to become more project and proactively orientated.

Strategies For A More Proactive Operation

The Special Staff Meeting

The simple goal of the November 1976 staff meeting was to reduce casework and with the resources thus freed to adopt a more proactive approach. One of the initial decisions taken was that in future no case could be accepted by UCLC for detailed advice and assistance unless a 'sponsor' had first presented the facts of the case to one of the weekly staff meetings. The sponsor – a UCLC employee or a volunteer worker – would have to convince those present that the case was deserving of further attention by a permanent member of staff. Concomitantly, the number of cases receiving oral advice only was to be increased and clients were to be encouraged to do much more for themselves. Where oral advice and, for instance, encouraging the client to write to the relevant parties, were thought to be insufficient, the meeting decided that clients should then be referred to another agency or to one of the centre's own evening or weekend advice sessions. Here volunteer lawyers could provide the necessary support. However, volunteers themselves were to be instructed to reduce severely the number of cases received at advice sessions that were subsequently referred to salaried members of staff as cases deserving of detailed advice and assistance. Henceforth, volunteer solicitors would need the approval of the salaried duty lawyer – a permanent UCLC employee – before any volunteer could either accept a case himself for detailed work or refer it to a staff meeting for consideration as a case worthy of such treatment. Moreover, these 'internal referrals' would also require a sponsor at the weekly staff meetings, and their ultimate acceptance or rejection would depend on decisions taken by these meetings.

All clients eligible for Legal Aid were to be referred to private practitioners unless their cases were considered to be of particular importance or the clients involved needed special support from UCLC staff. Where possible clients were to be encouraged to conduct their own cases and to solve their own problems. To facilitate self–help outcomes of this kind it was decided to produce a range of explanatory leaflets for use by clients. The November meeting also stressed the importance of substantially increasing the educational and project work of the centre. Finally, the staff decided to request that the centre remain closed on Thursday mornings in addition to Thursday afternoons so that more time could be made available to prepare leaflets and to plan and implement projects. The centre's management committee agreed to this request shortly after the November meeting.

Nearly two years later in October 1978, at the end of my study of UCLC, the centre had failed to implement most of the decisions taken at the November 1976 meeting. The operational activities of the centre did not change markedly, despite the fact that there was some reduction in the number of individual cases in this period. The fact of this reduction, but no corresponding increase in proactive activities, suggests that while the caseload level is an important element in any attempt to become more proactively orientated, it is not the only factor. Bellow (1977:56), for instance, has found that even in agencies with relatively low caseloads proactive treatment of cases does not necessarily occur. He attributed this to the way in which professional attitudes among lawyers are both formed and justified. In particular, Bellow criticized the failure of legal education to equip lawyers with the necessary skills, confidence, and perspectives to advocate the collective interests of poor clients. In his view many law centre lawyers see high caseloads as providing an excuse or 'a legitimate reason why they cannot thoroughly prepare and investigate cases or link them to local organising efforts to exert political pressure' (Bellow, 1977:57). Too often, argued Bellow, the lawyer working for poor people has followed accepted professional attitudes and defined his intervention in their problems in narrow legal terms. This is to overlook the possibilities of linking legal strategies to community–based political efforts and, indirectly, it also serves to justify 'the limited approach to individual client grievances' (Bellow, 1977:58).

Some evidence for Bellow's line of argument can be seen in some of the quotations taken from various UCLC annual reports, and in the views of the centre's lawyers, one of whom told me that:

'It's difficult to redirect things once we'd started up as a casework agency. It's difficult to keep casework under control. Cases can only be related to one another. If you justify taking on one case it's difficult to avoid taking on similar cases. There is still not sufficient priority given to educational and community work; this is so because of the demands of casework. Solicitors feel these demands particularly, especially me, since I've the greatest casework background. You must meet deadlines, appear in court. You have to do these things or be sued for negligence. It's difficult to change approach from casework to educational and community work'.

The difficulties of changing the centre's approach persisted throughout 1977 and 1978. In – service training sessions started and the centre remained closed all day on Thursdays, and there was a gradual reduction in the number of cases. However, while this reduction was reflected in subsequent annual reports, it was not apparent to the staff in the months immediately following November 1976. They still had high caseloads with which to cope, and they still had new cases to accept – albeit under a new procedure. Not surprisingly they found that the servicing of individual cases was still taking up the vast majority of their time and that no project work was getting under way. Little had changed and, gradually, the optimism surrounding the November meeting ebbed away as staff found that they were still subject to heavy pressures, such as the need to service the increased numbers of people requiring advice at the reception desks and the continuing demands of time – consuming individual casework.

At the end of 1977, in a further attempt to reduce casework and to become more proactively orientated, the centre decided to reorganize itself into three units: housing, family, and employment. While this plan was being implemented several staff members felt that it was also a good time to review the whole of the centre's operation and to question why the decisions of the November 1976 meeting had not been successfully followed through. Accordingly, after further discussions on this issue, in May 1978 one of the centre's lawyers and a general worker were asked to investigate. At the same time, the staff felt that it would be appropriate to conduct an appraisal of the unit reorganization, which by then had been in place for several months. Each unit, therefore, was asked to produce a report highlighting its current work and indicating future initiatives. The review, the reports of the units, and some other individual contributions were to show clearly the difficulties encountered by a reactive centre such as UCLC as it tried to adopt a more proactive orientation.

The joint report of the lawyer and general worker stated that all staff had been disappointed in the results of the November 1976 meeting.

The cases were indeed cut down but projects were not getting off the ground. It seemed we had overlooked two factors.
1. Casework will always expand to fill any time available.
2. Project work needs an enormous amount of effort, co – ordination and co – operation. It does not come 'naturally' out of casework, it usually cannot be done effectively by one member of staff working in isolation (UCLC, 1978a:7 – 8).

Thus, while staff were supposed on Thursdays to employ their time in the preparation of leaflets and projects, free from the attentions of the general public, in practice many of them were using this period to catch up on the demands of existing individual casework. In a paper presented at a staff meeting in June 1977 one of the centre's lawyers concluded that:

No one could argue that closing on Thursday mornings has been an unmitigated success so far as training and group work activity is concerned. It has given us a bit more time to catch up on casework. We have had some useful inservice training sessions, and a lot of time has been wasted. Hardly any leaflets have come near to fruition (UCLC, June 1977:3).

There was a general view among the staff that while the centre's casework had become more rational and was better structured by the centre's operational priorities for case acceptance, the centre had not adopted a significantly more proactive approach. With the exception of the kind of work the centre was doing in schools, it had generally failed to initiate any new projects, and the centre certainly did not attempt to organize individuals into coherent groups. Instead it responded from time to time to ad hoc requests from existing local groups for information on particular topics. In short, the community work role of UCLC occupied an ambiguous position. On the one hand, it was viewed as the provision of legal information and advice to local groups, a function exactly the same at the centre's educational work in schools. On the other hand, there was some awareness that community work also potentially involved the active formation of local groups. However, this latter view had never been operationalized at UCLC whose preferred approach was as follows:

In contrast to other models of community work where the community worker's role is to go out into the community and search out groups they perceive as needing organisation, the preferred practice of the Law Centre is to intervene on issues that arise through legal casework (UCLC, March 1976:5).

Ironically this practice could not be pursued to its limit because the very fact of heavy caseloads prevented UCLC from devoting sufficient resources to its community work functions. Indeed, this particular deficiency of the reactive stance has been acknowledged by UCLC staff who stated that the centre needed 'to control the way

57

the work comes to us before we can hope to develop group work on the scale which it deserves and which the problems of the community demand' (UCLC, 1978a:6).

The intermittent contact with local groups, the disappointingly low level of project and community work, the general failure to implement the decisions of the November 1976 meeting, and an awareness of the frustrations associated with an overly reactive approach were all behind the reorganization of UCLC into units at the end of 1977. This constituted a further attempt to develop project work.

Unit Reorganization

The housing, employment, and family units each contained at least one lawyer and a general worker – the housing unit contained two lawyers reflecting the preponderance of such work in the locality. It had become increasingly clear to the staff 'that from the beginning of the law centre, there [had] been a contradiction between our way of working and our wish to be more active in the crucial area of group work' (UCLC, 1978a:5). While unit reorganization fell short of resolving the fundamental question of what should be UCLC's basic operational philosophy, it was nevertheless intended to be a means by which the centre could adopt more progressive policies. In essence, the intention of the reorganization was to allow staff 'to share more easily the skills and knowledge necessary for the group, project and education work' (UCLC, 1977–8:3). This was, therefore, an attempt both to overcome the previous isolation of individual members of staff who were planning project work, and to develop the coordination and cooperation between them, which would be essential to the successful introduction of a more proactive style.

By June 1978 the reports from the centre's three units were available for discussion. The housing unit recommended in its paper that no new cases be taken on in future unless they were directly relevant to the aims and contents of existing and proposed housing projects. A separate report prepared by one of the housing unit's lawyers described the unit's only example of project work that had been concluded at that time. It involved a reduction in rates for tenants on a housing estate following a successful court case. The same paper described too the unit's preparatory work on a pamphlet dealing with flat – sharing, and its negotiations with the local authority's housing committee to try to find a more satisfactory procedure for handling council tenants' rent arrears than the issuing of summonses. A paper by a general worker from the housing unit highlighted the preparatory work on another pamphlet dealing with rent payments, and it also described the involvement of two students on placement at UCLC in a repairs project. The unit as a whole was interested in pursuing cases of disrepair under s.99 of the Public Health Act 1936, and a student on placement was exploring the advantages of preparing a leaflet on the procedure under this section. The leaflet was intended for use by UCLC staff and not for distribution to clients. Two other students in the centre had started work on a 'repairs kit' to be used primarily as an information sheet for those working at UCLC. The kit was to contain in one handy package the relevant legislation on repairs, which was to be collated from diverse sections of various public health and housing acts; it would also outline the different procedures to be followed.

Most of the activities being undertaken at this time by the housing unit did not significantly involve the direct and active participation of clients. Moreover, the pamphlets and projects under preparation were heavily oriented towards legal procedures and legal outcomes with little apparent scope for a combination of non – legal and legal strategies. Furthermore, much of the work was dependent on students. The family unit, to give another example, outlined some of its future initiatives and then warned that these would be dependent on volunteers. Finally, the staff of the employment unit expressed the view that they had insufficient resources to implement successfully the proposals they had in mind.

The reports and papers from the three units indicated a range of new initiatives, which appeared to augur well for the future. Indeed, the idea of the law centre being organized into units took a firm hold and in 1979 a race and immigration unit was added to the original three. In 1982 a welfare rights worker was appointed, bringing the total number of units to five, which reflected not only the continuity of some problem areas but also the emergence of new issues. However, unit reorganization did not produce immediate results. In 1978 only the housing unit had actually implemented any projects. The other units were simply voicing ideas on which projects they intended to start work, and in the meanwhile they continued to service individual cases. However, my own research at UCLC ended a few months after unit reorganization and, thus, I am not able to provide a detailed empirical analysis of this development. What does appear to have happened however, judging from UCLC's subsequent annual reports, is that project work has become a more noticeable feature of the activities of its units.

For example, the housing unit has undertaken advice work with a local housing aid centre and with residents' associations. The immigration unit, in addition to the large amount of individual casework it handles, has also been involved with local and national groups dealing with immigration policy. The welfare rights unit, another sector of the law centre facing tremendous demands for individual advice has, nevertheless, conducted some outreach work with a small number of community – based groups. The employment unit has prioritized certain types of cases in which it is prepared to act for individuals, and has developed some non – casework activities by cooperating with local groups on specific issues such as low pay. The family unit with its emphasis on care and custody proceedings, juvenile crime, and educational rights not surprisingly still conducts most of its work at the individual casework level. Indeed, despite the examples given, UCLC itself remains as a predominantly reactive law centre, with an open – door emphasis, which means that the 'demand for advice and casework has continued unabated' (UCLC, 1984 – 6:1). Thus, whatever other needs the group and project work of the centre may be satisfying, it is not producing any reduction in the number of individuals requiring the centre's services. In fact, the 'calls from the local community for advice and free legal representation continue to increase' (UCLC, 1986 – 7:i).

It would seem that despite the reorganization of the centre into units, UCLC still suffers severe caseload problems as a result of its open – door reactive approach. The progress that UCLC has made in terms of widening the extent and variety of its non – casework activities has proved to be a slow and, at times, frustrating experience. Moreover, part of this progress was probably related to the decision in the early 1980s to close the centre to the public on Tuesdays as well as Thursdays. In a review of the original unit reorganization one of the centre's general workers argued that:

Individual casework has continued to dominate the time and energy of workers here, and although we have cut down considerably on the number of cases, it has not been possible to take on project work in its place. Inevitably, it happens that the more time is available for each individual case, the more fully it is gone into. And so, while individuals may have been rather better served, this has been at a cost of assisting more clients. Also, it necessarily happens that project work must inevitably take second place to deadlines imposed continually by casework; and we have not had the time available to have the necessary discussions with groups in the community with whom we would like to work more closely. Although in 1976, we were strongly in favour of keeping the door open four and a half days per week, our experience since then has shown that this, too, has been a major barrier to expanding our project work. The open door necessitates each worker spending at least one, often two, half days actually participating in the reception rota. But the real cost in terms of time is much greater. The lawyers in particular find that they are frequently called upon to answer questions arising from the reception desk at all times the centre is open to the public. Again, the immediate query always tends to take precedence over more long term work we are attempting to do (UCLC, June 1978:5).

Given this predominant and persistent emphasis on the reactive delivery of legal services to UCLC's clients, what did this approach achieve in terms of securing citizenship rights, providing informed consent, enhancing client competence, and establishing party upgrading?

If any law centre is to provide high levels of informed consent and to develop client competence, it must spend time with clients and encourage them to become actively involved in pursuing solutions to their problems. The extent to which reactive law centres in general and UCLC in particular can expend resources on such goals depends crucially on the level of individual cases. Since caseloads are almost invariably very heavy within reactive law centres and put staff and resources under severe pressure, there is a tendency for most individual cases to be handled in a relatively routine fashion. In addition to the actual number of cases, which a reactive law centre has to handle, there are three other major characteristics contributing to this tendency towards routine treatment. These are the kinds of problems that low – income clients bring to the law centre; the processes adopted by the centre to achieve certain remedies; and the nature of the remedies available.

Problems

The problems received by UCLC and other reactive centres are closely associated with the socio – economic status of their clientele. Reactive law centres in inner – city areas attract clients whose ranks are heavily populated by the low – paid, the unemployed, single – parent families, the old, and ethnic minorities. UCLC as a typical reactive centre services those groups in British society that experience the greatest difficulties in securing decent housing, adequate welfare provision, or equitable treatment from any number of agencies. Most clients arrive at UCLC in a relatively unscreened manner. On arrival at reception desks they are divided into clients who may be referred elsewhere, clients who need advice – only, or clients requiring more detailed attention.

This last category, where a case file is opened, does not frequently include cases that involve crucial issues of policy and important points of law. For the most part, clients come to UCLC with problems that, while obviously important to each individual, typically relate to localized issues. Few cases have far – reaching consequences and, unlike wealthy individuals and private corporations that often require preventive and anticipatory legal assistance, UCLC clients more usually approach the centre when their problems are at or nearing crisis point. Such cases are rarely able to influence the policies of public and private institutions. Thus,

> the demands brought by poor clients do not require the legal aid lawyer to develop responses significant to many others beyond the immediate present clientele. Legal aid lawyers are expected not to grow beyond the local social environment. This is indicated by pressures for summary treatment of cases from adversaries, courts and clients. Summary treatment requires a minimum of research and other preparatory activities (Katz, 1976:6).

This state of affairs is only partially offset by the work of UCLC with local and national groups on wider policy issues and by its pursuit of occasional 'test' cases, which may have a broader impact and obviously require detailed preparation. In general, the limited applicability and consequentiality of most individual cases are influential factors in the tendency towards routine treatment.

Processes

Problems taken to a reactive centre are referred elsewhere, handled by way of oral advice, or are taken on as cases requiring more detailed attention. Referral elsewhere, while it may be in the client's best interests, is often a routine matter. UCLC is fortunate in that in the years following its opening a number of local solicitors have become more willing to take on areas of work referred from the law centre. Other advice agencies in the locality have become more specialized and they too are now better able to deal with referrals (UCLC, 1984:6). Most referred and advice – only cases were 'one – shot' encounters in the sense that clients were passing through UCLC and were not about to form lengthy professional – client relationships. Advice – only cases between receptionists and those who had called into the centre were relatively brief, usually lasting less than fifteen minutes during the period of my research at UCLC. Since that time, however, the centre decided to provide more detailed advice wherever possible and it wished to increase the time spent with advice – only clients to between thirty minutes and an hour per encounter. Although I cannot say for certain, it may be that this current approach to advice – only cases at UCLC has minimized much of the former routinized nature of professional – client encounters at the reception desks. However, even with a somewhat more detailed approach to advice – giving, there are limits to what one can expect in terms of developing client competence and self – help outcomes.

In most cases where clients were expected and encouraged to take some self – help form of action, this was usually limited to clients writing their own letters to other relevant parties. Most clients appeared to be very appreciative simply to have had their legal position explained to them, even if at times the position was a hopeless one. My own research at UCLC confirmed the observations of Katz (1976:17) who in his study of agencies employing lawyers to help the poor reported that 'the vast majority of clients met on intake require no more than routine treatment'. This view was also reflected in the attitudes of the staff at UCLC. Although reception desk duties could be time – consuming and might disrupt other work in progress, the problems presented by clients were for the most part perceived as falling into routine categories.

However, it was not simply advice – only and referral cases that had a limited consequentiality for UCLC staff; cases taken on for more detailed treatment could also be somewhat routinely processed. As Katz has noted:

In the kind of preparation they put into a case, lawyers indicate their appreciation of its complexities and their need to grow to respond. Counselling clients, drafting documents, negotiating or trying a case and orally arguing in court are defined as challenging occasions for improving and testing competence when they are approached through extensive preparation. Indicators of preparation include internal memos, multiple or painstaking drafts, consultation over strategy, rehearsals for in – court performances, investigation of facts, creation of evidence by depositions and interrogatories and preparation of witnesses. The definition overwhelmingly applied to preparatory tasks by the social environment most immediate to the legal aid lawyer is that they are inappropriate. Directly or indirectly, the courts in which clients are sued, the adversaries with whom they have been struggling, their lawyers, and clients at legal aid themselves call for summary treatment of the problems presented to the legal aid lawyer (Katz, 1976:8 – 9).

It was not that UCLC employees did not do any of these preparatory tasks; rather that cases where such a range of activities took place were relatively few. Internal memoranda relating to particular cases were uncommon as indeed were consultations between lawyers who, on the contrary, tended to concentrate on their own individual caseloads. Multiple drafts of strategies were equally uncommon, and there were few rehearsals for court performance other than those of general applicability conducted at training sessions. On the other hand, the creation of evidence, although subject to large variation, could occasionally be extensive. However, the preparation of witnesses, not unreasonably, only became a priority if it appeared that an actual case might go to court. Few cases offered exciting legal challenges or required new legal ground to be explored in depth.

Remedies

For many clients, especially if they were seeking an explanation of their legal position, the giving of advice by UCLC staff was often a satisfactory remedy. Where clients were expected to engage in some form of self – help activity or were referred elsewhere it is impossible to say whether these constituted effective remedies, for the clients involved had essentially ceased to be UCLC clients and were now reliant either upon themselves or upon some other agency to find a solution to their problems. With cases taken on for more detailed processing, the position was somewhat clearer. There was a distinct tendency during the period of my research at UCLC for the centre to favour negotiated settlements. Only a small proportion of housing cases, for instance, actually went to court, but of those that did eviction proceedings were obviously cases of crucial importance.

UCLC, however, was often powerless and found that such cases were frequently a matter of

> having to explain to the client what rights he or she does have, what is involved in the proceedings being taken against him or her, what can or cannot be done as regards rehousing by the local authority and preparing them for the inevitability of having to search for a new home. Very often it was found we were attending at the Rent Tribunal to ask for a period of security, then finally providing representation at the County Court proceedings to ask for yet further time – all of which was designed to simply buy time for the local authority housing department before they had to make a decision on rehousing; which decision is not in any case made until the tenant has actually had a court order for possession made against him or her (UCLC, 1974:3).

Even when UCLC took a case to court and won, the eventual outcome for the client might still be unsatisfactory, as the problems of housing disrepair clearly show. The centre was concerned about the difficulties of enforcing the legal rights of clients who lived in unfit properties (UCLC, 1974 – 5:7 – 8), and noted that:

> The argument that the landlord cannot pay has been used over and over again to deny our clients basic repairs, and one of the worst aspects of this is the landlord who cannot pay is as likely to be the Council as it is the private landlord (UCLC, 1975 – 6:11 – 12).

The range and adequacy of the remedies pursued by UCLC might have been improved had the centre attempted to combine legal and non – legal strategies in a concerted and committed fashion. However, such a proactive approach was not tried and the centre relied in the main on legal activities and outcomes.

Thus it was that at UCLC there was a combination of factors responsible for the tendency towards routine treatment, not least the sheer volume of work taken on by the centre. The high level of cases led to staff frustration and disillusionment concerning the impact of the centre's work and its often routine nature. Other factors helped to compound the routine processing of individual cases. Indeed, this routine processing of cases and the concomitant absence of group and project work, which the staff felt would provide a more personally challenging as well as a more effective set of activities, were major influences on the decision to call the November 1976 staff meeting and on the subsequent unit reorganization of the centre. In addition to their consequences for the job satisfaction of the staff, the open – door reactive stance of UCLC and the extent of routine case processing also had implications for clients.

Clients, Competence, And Participation

As well as being a reactive law centre, UCLC also exhibited some elements of the 'bureaucratic' approach. The centre had, in theory, a commitment to providing services for all of the indigent people living within its catchment area. The fact that it did not achieve a fully comprehensive coverage does not detract from this emphasis upon equity between potential clients. Insufficient resources and a lack of knowledge about the centre among potential clients in more outlaying districts of the borough prevented UCLC from completely fulfilling this goal. Nonetheless, it did operate on the basis of attempting to distribute scarce resources in a rational and equitable manner; services were given based on individual need and not on the basis of an individual's membership or otherwise of an organized group. UCLC was also bureaucratic in the sense that, with the exception of its work with schools, its services were in the main centrally located.

After the initial setting up of the centre, it was the staff of UCLC who took the major responsibility for persisting with the original services or modifying them in some manner. Client involvement in the management of the services of UCLC was indirect rather than direct. Client influence took the form, for the most part, of expressed satisfaction, or occasionally dissatisfaction, with the services they received. Clients were not directly or actively involved in the detailed plans of the centre's staff to develop, modify, or alter UCLC's services. Unlike large scale bureaucracies in the social welfare area, many of the criticisms applied to them were not applicable to UCLC. For instance, UCLC staff, the employees of an agency with 'bureaucratic' tendencies, could hardly be said to have failed to comply with the main goal set for the centre by its funding agent, the local council. Although the professional staff had an interest in trying to modify the way in which the centre operated, they did not as a group seek to subvert the centre's original goal of providing an open–door legal advice service to the poor of the area.

Large scale public welfare bureaucracies have also been criticized for distributing resources inefficiently and ineffectively, partly as a result of these agencies' lack of accountability, and partly as a result of the job security of their employees. At UCLC, however, such a charge in the light of the continuous staff commitment, dedication, and expertise would appear most harsh. These same public welfare bureaucracies have also been criticized for failing to involve their own employees in decision–making. At UCLC it was the employees themselves, rather than the local council or the centre's management committee, who gave serious detailed thought to the centre's operation, and to how it might be improved for the benefit of staff and clients alike.

Another criticism of welfare bureaucracies is that they do not involve the consumers of their services in direct participation in the management of those services. To some extent this is true of UCLC but to leave the point there would be to overlook those 'participatory' emphases that existed alongside the bureaucratic ones at the centre. In contrast to the bureaucratic approach where there tends to be a well – defined and somewhat rigid staff hierarchy, this was much less noticeable at UCLC. Although it began operations with a legal director and relatively strict demarcation lines between solicitors, secretaries, and other kinds of non – legal staff, within a few years these lines had blurred. The centre's director had left and was not replaced; the non – legal workers became known as general workers and were increasingly responsible for their own caseloads. Despite the acknowledged pre – eminence of legal personnel in the legal sphere, the UCLC staff worked on a cooperative and relatively democratic basis with little of the inflexibility associated with rigid staff roles.

As regards the issue of accountability, UCLC staff felt that they were accountable to their funding agent in the sense that they provided a service according to the rules and guidelines within which they had to operate. They also argued that they were accountable to clients in the sense that all staff were committed to maintaining and improving client satisfaction with the services offered. While clients had little or no say in deciding the nature and content of these services, nevertheless, there were indications of a somewhat more participatory emphasis in respect of individual relationships between clients and staff. This participatory emphasis was most marked in cases requiring detailed attention and preparation. The most fruitful way to discuss this issue is to analyse the nature of the professional – client relationships at UCLC, and which are typical of relationships at similar reactively orientated law centres.

At the level of client involvement in the management of the centre's operations during the period of my research at UCLC, there was little direct consumer participation other than by those lay people (former clients) who sat on the centre's management committee. The rather minimal role of these individuals at that time was summarized by the centre as follows:

> Representatives from official bodies often unwittingly dominate [management committee] discussions because they are more used to the kinds of discussion taking place and because they have more professional knowledge. Community representatives often need a slower education into the working and running of the law centre than has been available so far (UCLC, 1977 – 8:4).

The role of community representatives in the running of law centres was an issue addressed by the Royal Commission on Legal Services whose report I shall discuss in detail in a later chapter.

At the level of defining the nature of the client's problem, there was similarly little participation in the lawyer – client relationship by the client. It was the professional who normally defined the legal dimension of the problem brought by the client to the centre. This is hardly surprising given the pressure on staff to process so many cases. In these circumstances it is both quicker and more efficient for the UCLC employee to formulate the nature of client grievances than to leave it to individual clients to try to come up with an accurate legal definition. Such a phenomenon is in keeping with Johnson's (1972) notion of the professionalist control of the practitioner – client relationship. At UCLC and at other similar reactive law centres, the normal practitioner – client relationship is one that is largely controlled by the professional. Thus, although the relationship is client initiated, it is the professional who determines its one – to – one nature, and it is the professional who terminates the relationship in most instances.

The crucial aspect of professionalist control, however, is that it is the professional who defines the needs of the client and the manner in which those needs will be met. The first aspect, the definition of need, is firmly in the control of UCLC staff, and not unreasonably so. The advantage of staff control is that the client will receive a competent, focused, and relevant service. It also allows the professional to employ his time and resources in the most efficient manner. The second aspect of professionalist control is not so straightforward.

It would be wrong to say that having defined the legal dimension of the client's problem, reactive law centre lawyers then proceed to impose a course of action on the client. While it is often true that in many cases only one relevant or appropriate course of action is available to lawyer and client, even here the cooperation and consent of the client would be actively sought. This process of informed consent, based on a full explanation of the legal position and the consequences of a certain course of action, is most pronounced in those cases that are more complex, or that involve decisions of principle, which must be taken by the client. For instance, such decisions of principle would include whether a client was willing potentially to allow his case to proceed to court; whether he wished to make a claim for compensation in addition to the original grievance; whether he wanted to have repairs effected to his home or to take alternative accommodation; and so on. With such decisions the client plays an important, active, and participatory role. Clients essentially reserve their rights to take decisions on vital matters of principle or personal standing.

Informed consent and people – working techniques are crucial dimensions of client participation in such decisions. People – working techniques relate information to the client about his legal position and his possible legal avenues of redress. At UCLC and other reactive law centres the professionals use their knowledge to help clients but they do not often relate clients' problems to the wider socio – economic context, which more fully developed people – working techniques would attempt to do. This 'political' dimension of many clients' problems is largely avoided in most professional – client relationships. Indeed, few actual clients ever express a desire to move beyond the specific legal dimensions of their immediate problems. It is difficult for clients to recognize any direct benefits that may flow from any attempt to contextualize their individual problems within a wider socio – economic analysis and framework for action. In like manner, few clients recognize any benefits that might stem from being directly involved in the processing of their cases.

As the legal position is explained to them, as they exercise decisions of principle over the broad conduct of the case, so the legal competence of clients and their awareness of law and legal rights are increased. But this is a long way from having the technical expertise to process a case oneself. Clients recognize the professional authority of law centre staff in the sphere of technical expertise to proceed without the direct participation of themselves. In so far as the technical preparation and processing of cases are concerned, most clients take the view that the professional 'knows best'. While this may be perfectly appropriate, it does mean that the competence of clients, where it is significantly increased at all, is limited to the legal dimension. Reactive law centres, such as UCLC, rarely explore the 'political' dimensions of clients' problems, nor do they often develop party upgrading for the simple reason that reactive law centres tend to concentrate in the main on servicing individual cases.

Moreover, we should not assume that all individual cases involve significant levels of informed consent and improved legal competence for clients. Most cases require advice – only, or are referred elsewhere, and here the scope for active client participation, the exercise of informed consent, and the development of legal competence are severely curtailed. In many cases, clients occupied a generally passive role in the professional – client relationship and, whatever rights and tangible benefits may have come their way, clients were not often actively engaged in seeking them. On the contrary, they were frequently the passive recipients of the rights of citizenship, which had been secured on their behalf by lawyers and others at reactive law centres.

The reactive delivery of legal services is one route towards the realization of citizenship rights; proactive law centres provide another route. The proactive orientation, like its reactive counterpart, also seeks to realize rights. However, it adopts rather different strategies and aspires to different goals from those common within reactive law centres, and it is to those issues that I now turn my attention.

Notes

1.	In the period April 1974 to March 1975 UCLC referred 1,760 persons to other agencies, of which 772 (43.3%) were to private solicitors. It received 657 referrals from outside agencies, of which 25 (3.81%) came from private practitioners. Between April 1975 and March 1976 1,537 referrals were made by the centre; 684 (44.5%) going to private solicitors. According to the 1986 – 7 annual report, UCLC referred in that period 3,760 cases to CABx and other agencies, and an additional 1,890 to private solicitors. As one would expect of a reactive law centre having to cope with increasing demands for its services, the 1987 – 8 report shows yet another increase in referrals; 4,830 cases being referred to CABx and other agencies, and 2,260 to private solicitors.

2. See Sheffield City Polytechnic Sociolegal Studies Group (1978:15), which reported that in its sample of 231 clients 78% of recommended referrals to solicitors actually took place.

3. In later years the centre added immigration and nationality, and welfare rights advice to its areas of concern.

4. The opening of another law centre in the locality a few years later relieved UCLC of its duty to provide a service for the whole of the borough.

5. The demands on the centre have grown steadily over the years so that in the year 1987 – 8 there were 35,310 contacts made with UCLC. Of these, 9,210 were personal callers at the centre, and 26,100 were telephone calls. The total number of cases taken on by its various units in this period was 2,109.

   Some idea of the volume of individual callers and of telephone enquiries, both of which are handled by the two staff of reception desk duty, may be gained from the following information. In one particular day (on which detailed records were kept) in 1974 UCLC received 151 telephone calls and 84 people visited the centre. For three consecutive days in April 1976 when records of telephone calls were kept, they numbered respectively 108, 132, and 149.

6. These 'outreach' training activities with the staff of other advice agencies involved housing aid and women's centre workers.

7. The centre noted that right from its opening large numbers of people were calling into the centre or telephoning for advice, so much so that the centre's solicitors and support staff were soon severely overworked (UCLC, 1974 – 5:2).

5 The potential for a proactive alternative

As I mentioned towards the end of Chapter Three, much of the proactive philosophy that influenced the work of Britain's small number of proactive law centres could be found within the pages of *Towards Equal Justice*. When it was published in 1974 there existed only a handful of law centres. *Towards Equal Justice* in some respects represented a clarion call to the emerging law centre movement to adopt a more thorough proactive approach[1]. Even so, the majority of law centres at their inception continued to be structured along reactive lines. Moreover, as the examples in the previous chapter indicate, the same centres encountered severe difficulties in trying to modify significantly their reactive styles of operation in favour of a more proactive stance. The British law centre movement has only ever contained a small number of law centres with a significantly proactive style of operation. Their importance does not therefore inhere in their geographical coverage of the country, nor in the numbers of clients for whom they provide a service; rather their importance lies both in the radically different manner in which they deliver legal *and non-legal* services, and in the different kind of relationship that they try to forge with clients. I shall first give some brief examples of the proactive approach as adopted by Adamsdown, Newham, and Brent law centres[2], before moving on to a detailed case-study of the work of the Northern Neighbourhood Law Centre.

The Work And Goals Of Proactive Law Centres

Adamsdown

Adamsdown Law Centre is an agency that has enjoyed some success in adopting a more proactive approach despite its open – door policy. Like Brent and the Northern law centres, which owed their origins to various initiatives by groups of local inhabitants, Adamsdown 'grew out of a number of small community projects undertaken by members of Cardiff University in the late 1960s, and it was developed as a body capable of initiating a range of projects and services for local people' (Adamsdown Community Trust, 1978:5). While it has always been prepared to deal with individual cases, the centre's staff have recognized from the start of their work that there is also an important need to provide legal and non – legal services to local groups. Such services are provided at Adamsdown where it has been recognized that:

> Legal problems often overlap with social problems and those of local and central government policy. It is therefore necessary for the team of staff to work together on these issues, pooling their various skills so as to overcome the obstacles to success...(Adamsdown Community and Advice Centre, 1975:5).

Even with problems such as that of housing disrepair where there are various legal avenues of redress, the centre found that despite servicing large numbers of individual cases the problem of disrepair persisted in the locality. It was for this reason that a substantial portion of the time of the staff was given over to legal work on group issues. These groupwork activities have been pursued with some success; indeed, the centre was responsible for an innovative use of the Green Form scheme in its successful attempt to improve the condition of roads and pavements in the area (Adamsdown Community and Advice Centre, Summer 1976). Adamsdown's employment of a welfare rights worker, a full – time community worker, a part – time community worker, and a part – time research and development officer enabled it to devote important resources and skills to groupwork projects in addition to those provided by the centre's legal personnel. Moreover, its catchment area conferred a crucial advantage not enjoyed by other open – door centres. The population of the catchment area was approximately 10,000 people,

> which leaves the Centre with the highest ratio of staff resources to population of all the existing Law Centres. This enables the Centre to have a high caseload per head of population served but also to have sufficient resources to work with groups of residents who experience common difficulties (Adamsdown Community Trust, 1978:5 – 6).

Adamsdown Law Centre was conceived with the intention that its resources be used for proactive undertakings. Despite its open – door policy the centre was able to make a reality of that concept because of its small catchment area in relation to staff resources, which meant that proactive work was not extensively undermined by the need to service individual cases.

Newham

Newham Rights Centre was created as an agency with very firm proactive goals. The planning of the centre, which took place in 1973, noted the difficulties that North Kensington had experienced in the previous three years with its open – door, reactive structure. The whole point of recognizing those difficulties was not to plan a reactive centre that could avoid most of the caseload problems, but to plan a proactive centre *with a completely different delivery system and set of goals*. Indeed, Newham Rights Centre was funded in September 1973 by the Nuffield Foundation's Legal Advice and Assistance programme with the express intention that the centre become an innovatory 'socio – legal centre'. The term 'socio – legal' indicated that the centre 'was not to restrict itself to purely legal problems, but to concern itself with the overlapping nature of people's social and legal needs. However, the Foundation agreed to leave the precise details of philosophy and approach to the staff of the centre' (Newham Rights Centre, 1974 – 5:7). The staff had already had an opportunity to address the centre's approach prior to its opening in January 1974 since they had been involved in the formulation of *Towards Equal Justice*. However, the centre's philosophy was most clearly set out in the report of the centre's first fifteen months of operation, in which it was at pains to explain its policy in detail 'because it is one of the few Law Centres not committed to individual casework' (Newham Rights Centre, 1974 – 5:6).
The centre's staff argued that
a policy of funding only Law Centres which deal with individuals will mean that the lawyers in those Centres will be dealing with the same and similar problems for the same and similar individuals. This would continue indefinitely without any progress towards enabling people to deal with and prevent their problems themselves (Newham Rights Centre, 1974 – 5:6).
Unlike Brent Law Centre where local groups were involved from the outset in the planning and development of the centre, Newham was essentially an 'external' initiative, being an experimental programme funded by a particular charity. It took two years from the date of the centre's opening to set up a management committee composed of local inhabitants. Although Newham Rights Centre was committed to the idea of a community – based management committee, the reason for the delay in creating one was given as 'the need for the Centre to become established in the Borough first' (Newham Rights Centre, 1974 – 5:67). It was March 1976 – the centre eventually registering as an Industrial and Provident Society in September 1976 – before it 'assumed a democratic structure, consisting of a membership of representatives of local community

72

organisations. The members elected a Management Committee and that committee has been in effective control of the Centre since May 1976' (Newham Rights Centre, 1977:3).

The policy of the management committee has been a continuation of the original emphases to concentrate on group cases and 'test' cases, and to avoid individual casework wherever possible. The centre's main way of avoiding casework was to develop an efficient referral system and to inaugurate its own evening advice sessions staffed by volunteer solicitors and non – lawyers. Casework should normally only be taken on by salaried staff if a particular case is in keeping with the group and project work being undertaken by the centre. Sudden and dramatic increases in individuals bringing problems to the evening advice sessions obviously require some corresponding increase in the level of the centre's individual casework; but this is seldom the only measure adopted. Hence, when steep increases in gas, electricity and rent bills for local people meant that in a relatively short period of time there was a significant increase in the number of individuals unable to pay such bills, the centre was not content simply to carry out more casework and to refer clients in larger numbers to other agencies. In addition, the centre wrote *Debit and Credit*, a booklet that

has been extra – ordinarily well received and is used by both tenants associations and professional advisers. It has also been the subject of a series of workshops run in conjunction with the North East London Polytechnic and the Greater London Organisation of Citizens Advice Bureaux (Newham Rights Centre, 1977:6).

In order to service the levels of casework 'normally' occurring in the area the centre set up evening advice sessions. Most of the problems at these sessions required either advice – only or minimal assistance, and about 25% of cases were referred to local solicitors[3].

Newham's closed – door policy and its emphasis on group and educational cases have firmly positioned the centre towards the proactive end of the reactive – proactive continuum. Its operational philosophy may be summarized thus:

Instead of undertaking work on behalf of any person who happens to come through the door of the Law Centre, the Newham Rights Centre seeks out cases which have implications for more than just the individual involved. These cases are referred to the Centre by local organisations, local agencies, departments of the Local Authority and by the comprehensive network of contacts the Centre has built up in the Borough. In many instances such work is initiated by the staff of the Centre themselves. By taking cases directly involving numbers of people, or cases involving principles which affect numbers of people, the Law Centre is more likely to achieve permanent and lasting solutions to problems and to prevent recurrence of problems, than by tackling individual problems on an isolated and 'one – off' basis (Newham Rights Centre, 1974 – 5:8).

In keeping with this avowed intention the centre channels a significant part of its resources towards organizing local groups and advising existing ones. In this work the centre does not, however, rely on an overly legalistic approach, for as the Law Centres' Federation has stated:

It is important to appreciate the necessary balance of the workforce required before an agency can successfully carry out this defined preventative role. It cannot be done by a workforce dominated by those trained in law because this training leads to a narrow, precise and analytical way of thinking which (if a dominant feature of the law centre's attitude) is ill – suited to serving the expressions of communities as a whole. It is vital that those of the local community and workers skilled in community work are a strong component, numerically and ideologically in the centre if the capacity to identify and represent the demands of and the views of local communities is to be sufficiently contained within the resource (Law Centres' Federation, 1977:41).

While agreeing with such sentiments, Newham staff would no doubt add as a further justification for the proactive approach that 'organised groups can exert pressure in any number of ways on a whole range of public and private institutions, and in doing so, the use of the law is one tool amongst many, rather than the only and last resort of the unorganised...' (Newham Rights Centre, 1974 – 5:42).

Such an approach, in which individuals are encouraged to form coherent organized groups, may not only help to reduce unnecessary dependence on the skills and knowledge of lawyers, but also may provide opportunities to allow people to 'achieve the power to do things for themselves' (Newham Rights Centre, 1974 – 5:43). In the view of the staff at Newham, it is an entirely logical and appropriate step for the centre to become involved in the formation of local groups. For the law centre's personnel such a step is

the most effective means of distributing the limited resources of the Law Centre...Further it is only the power that comes with organisation that will really improve the conditions of the life of the underprivileged, and therefore legal services with that objective should adopt the approach of working with organisations (Newham Rights Centre, 1974 – 5:54).

In summary, it is evident that the work of Newham Rights Centre involves extensive interaction with the local community and community groups. Much of the work of the Centre can thus be described as community work.

The two principal community work functions for a Law Centre are:

74

(i)   encouragement and promotion of local and neighbourhood groups where none already exist, but with the aim that the people assisted should only have to rely on the Law Centre's skills for a short while so as to make the group self – supporting

(ii)   encouragement and assistance to local and neighbourhood groups to pursue courses of action they feel right and appropriate, but may not feel themselves competent enough to carry out (Newham Rights Centre, 1974 – 5:63).

Brent

The final brief example of a proactive law centre is that of Brent, which 'evolved' into a fully operational closed – door centre in 1973 from its origins in 1971 as a part – time advice agency. The advice centre had no permanent office and was staffed by a variety of legal and non – legal volunteers who concentrated on working with tenants' and residents' associations. It was during 1971 at a series of meetings attended by representatives of local tenants' groups, trades union branches and other local organizations, and a number of volunteer lawyers and non – lawyers that the idea of a law centre in Brent was developed. Brent Law Centre was from its outset to adopt a proactive approach with much emphasis on the active participation of clients. One of the main reasons for this was that during the discussions in which the centre was planned, it was agreed that

local groups and their representatives, rather than the staff, should determine what work the Centre would do, and, in particular, the basis on which this work would be selected. While this arrangement left to the staff full control over the manner in which they would conduct work for clients, it was intended by it to ensure that the work of the Centre – especially the lawyers – was in accordance with the aspirations of representatives of the sections of the community for whose benefit the Centre was intended – the 'consumers' of its services.

It was also decided that the Centre would not attempt to provide its services direct to the public. A main source of advice and assistance to the people of an area such as Brent was the local groups. It is to such a group that its members are likely to turn first in the event of a problem even if the problem is one outside the main scope of activity of the group. The legal profession could not hope to provide a substitute for this kind of help. By concentrating on working for and with local groups, and by trying to spread to the groups some of the professional knowledge of lawyers, the Centre could strengthen them by helping them both to function effectively as groups and to increase their ability to deal with problems raised by their individual members. It was intended that the cases for individuals handled directly by lawyers in the Centre would be cases of members of local groups which the groups could not handle themselves and which could not easily be dealt with by private solicitors. It was felt that close involvement of a local group in the cases handled by the Centre for its members would be a positive advantage in those cases. Further, by that time the North Kensington Neighbourhood Law Centre (the first and only then existing Law Centre) had already been overwhelmed by the demand for its services. It was hoped that the Brent Centre by working with local groups would be able to spread its resources as effectively as possible and, thereby, to avoid being quite so overwhelmed (Brent Community Law Centre, 1975:4 – 5).

Brent Law Centre has not avoided completely the problems of high individual caseloads but it has tried consistently to direct its resources predominantly towards proactive goals. Indeed, the centre has 'recognised that many of the problems facing people in a borough like Brent can be better tackled by providing legal services to groups and not just an individual service. Much of the work of the Centre is, therefore, the provision of help to people in groups' (Brent Community Law Centre, 1979:1). This group focus 'dates back to the founding of the Centre which occurred largely on the initiative of tenants' and residents' associations and trade union organisations assisted by a number of individuals' (Brent Community Law Centre, 1979:25)[4].

Given the group focus intended for the centre its staff were somewhat concerned by the unexpectedly large number of individual cases referred to them by various local agencies during the centre's first year of full – time operation in 1973 – 4. The volume of such cases was such that some projects intended to be carried out with local groups did not materialize. However, by the summer of 1974, the centre had brought individual case numbers under control and had even succeeded in reducing them[5].

The Centre has been cutting down on the numbers of individual cases it takes on and has been transferring the resources spent on them to group work.

The actual group work which the centre has carried out is nevertheless prodigious. We have assisted in the setting up of tenants associations, drafting constitutions for various groups, assisted in the preparation of agendas for and minutes of meetings, attended committee meetings, attended general meetings and public meetings, helped organise, and attended, conferences, advised on legal matters of interest to the groups, helped the groups in their relations with third parties, helped with their efforts to obtain funds and encouraged them to undertake joint projects. In all the centre has been concerned in the work of over 30 separate formally constituted local groups and at least as many informal or ad hoc groups. We estimate that between one third and one half of our resources have been engaged in this type of work (Brent Community Law Centre, 1975:21 – 2). Moreover, while working with groups always involves an 'educational' element, the above estimation did not include specific projects devoted to the legal education of various groups or agencies existing within the locality.

Brent Law Centre operates not as a 'front – line' agency servicing the needs of a succession of individuals, but as a 'resource' centre available both to local groups and to other advice – giving agencies in the area. Much of its work may be seen as an attempt to provide local people with the abilities to secure their rights without having to become over – reliant on lawyers. To achieve such a goal the centre tries to encourage the formation of self – help organizations for whom the centre can act as a 'resource', providing whatever services these groups may request (Brent Community Law Centre, 1976:1).

The factors that have influenced the creation and development of reactive law centres – and discussed earlier at the end of Chapter Two and in Chapter Three – are the same factors that apply to proactive centres. They are: the original organization of the centre; operational modifications made by staff or clients; levels of funding; and the nature of any 'external' components. It would be useful to discuss these factors in a general way in relation to the topic of segmentalism.

Law Centres And Segmentalism

The law centre movement as a whole may be seen as a distinct segment within the legal profession (Bucher and Strauss, 1960 – 1). Within that segment, however, there are a number of differences between the work of lawyers at reactive centres and the work of those at proactive agencies. For example, because of the group focus at proactive law centres, lawyers are more likely to be involved with greater frequency in direct cooperation with non – lawyers, such as community workers. In contrast, the tendency at reactive centres is for lawyers to become closely involved in processing individual clients' cases without recourse to cooperative relations with community workers.

There are also differences between the two types of law centre in terms of sense of mission and client milieux. In theory, at least, proactive lawyers are committed to a participatory relationship with their clientele as they seek to develop clients' organizational capabilities and competences. Reactive law centre lawyers, however, are less concerned with these factors, and are much more interested in the provision of access to legal services for individual citizens. There is a sense in which, in theory, and to some extent in practice, proactive and reactive lawyers form two sub – groups of what might be loosely called the salaried segment of the legal profession. The differences between the two sub – groups are not only explained in terms of variations in professional relationships and ideology, but also owe something to the operation of the four factors I identified a short while ago.

The first factor is the level of funding. While Adamsdown and Brent law centres were partly funded by local councils sympathetic to their respective styles of work, the Northern Law Centre was never able to attract such funds and had to exist on meagre resources donated by a number of charities. Newham Rights Centre was originally financed by a philanthropic foundation with the explicit intention of creating an innovative experiment in the delivery of legal and non – legal services[6]. The level and source of these funds played an important role in shaping the work of these few proactive law centres, both in terms of the amount of work they could undertake, and the kind of strategies they felt able to pursue.

Indeed, the whole issue of funding for proactive law centres is not just to do with the level of funds; it has become one of the 'external' factors helping to shape the role of such centres. Arguably, many potential funding bodies such as local councils are wary of what they perceive to be the 'political image' surrounding proactivity and proactive law centres. This second 'external' factor influencing the development of proactive law centres was a matter that was taken up by the Royal Commission on Legal Services, and it is one to which I shall return in later chapters.

The third factor in the work of proactive law centres is the nature of the initial planning and organization. While Newham was explicitly created with a proactive orientation, the proactive approach of the centres at Adamsdown, Brent, and Northern emerged from their respective original involvements with local groups. Both Brent and Northern developed into full – time proactive law centres from their earlier roles as part – time advice agencies helping to meet the needs of existing community groups. In contrast, agencies such as North Kensington, the Urban Community Law Centre, and many other reactive centres were set up in a more formal manner via the work of steering committees. It would seem that the dominating influence on such committees was that of the various professionals and the representatives of funding agencies. Their influence was directed towards the goal of opening law centres committed to providing individual access to legal services; the goal was rarely one of opening a centre devoted to the mobilization of local community groups and to the use of non – legal as well as legal strategies in a collective fashion. In general, steering committees drew up proposed reactive structures and operational philosophies for the law centres and then employed lawyers and others to implement them. At proactive law centres there is some evidence to suggest that legal and non – legal staff were more likely to have been original participants in the dialogue between the various professional and community interests that finally led to their formal establishment.

The final factor influencing the development of law centres is the extent to which staff and clients have been able to modify their operation. It would be best to address this topic in general terms by referring to the notion of community or communal control.

Community control of the general policies of law centres is an article of faith among the law centre movement and the Law Centres' Federation. However, attempts to make a reality of the concept through the creation of an effective management committee composed of representatives of the local clientele – the consumers of law centre services – have not always been successful. For instance, North Kensington Law Centre's attempt to set up a structure of community control was disappointing. Byles and Morris (1977:15) reported that too often management committee meetings were dominated by the legal personnel, which inhibited the contributions of lay members – the 'consumers'. Indeed, there has been much controversy within the movement as to whether any professionals or funding agency representatives should be allowed to sit on law centre management committees. Brent Law Centre takes the view that such people ought to be excluded if community control is to become a reality. While Brent has debarred membership for these kinds of individuals, other centres continue to include local councillors, representatives of local law societies, and other professional people so that there is a danger that the representatives of the local clientele may be outnumbered or feel inhibited by such a strong professional presence on management committees.

Even the remaining proactive centres with arguably the strongest commitment to community control have not always fared well in this area. The Northern Law Centre operated a system of 'checks and balances', where staff relied on their network of personal contacts in the community to judge whether they were remaining responsive to community needs and demands. But for many years it had no proper management committee and, thus, there could be no formal endorsement of nor expressed dissatisfaction with this system of checks and balances. Moreover, Newham Rights Centre essentially grafted on a management structure to its operations some years after those operations had been firmly laid down.

If one of the major ways that clients can express views about the future policies of their respective law centres is through the management committees of those centres, then it is imperative that the management committees do faithfully represent a system of community control. This is a topic I shall return to in later chapters. However, this initial discussion of community control and other relevant factors, coupled with a brief description of the work of Adamsdown, Brent, and Newham law centres, will have provided, I hope, a greater acquaintance with proactive themes and concepts in readiness for a detailed consideration of the role of the Northern Neighbourhood Law Centre (NNLC).

The Northern Neighbourhood Law Centre And The Potential Within The Community

Whereas in Chapter Four I argued that the experience and lessons of the Urban Community Law Centre were relevant in large measure to those of most other reactive law centres, I do not wish to claim the same for the Northern Law Centre. NNLC is not an operational metaphor for all other proactive law centres in Britain. This is because even with the small number of such centres there is great variation in their respective structures, levels of funding, origins, and so on. However, this case – study of NNLC can serve as a valuable insight into proactivity; how a proactive law centre tries to implement proactive concepts, and what difficulties such an agency faces. In short, NNLC gives us information about the extent to which, and under what conditions, a proactive law centre can help clients to realize some of the rights of citizenship.

The work of NNLC should not be seen, therefore, as the only or the best model for existing and future proactive law centres. Indeed, the centre no longer now exists as a law centre. The lessons drawn from this chapter, in which I shall cover in detail the work of NNLC in the housing field, will be applied to the debate concerning the future of the law centre movement and the goals that it should be pursuing. This will be the subject of the final chapter.

The Concept of Community

No discussion of the work of a proactive law centre can begin without first enquiring into the meaning of the term 'community', and examining the community work and action principles that guide much of the non – legal side of a proactive law centre's activities.

The term community can have three distinct meanings: a sense of belonging (affective, intrinsically – valued social relationships); locality (as in neighbourhood); and a particular target group that might serve as a vehicle for social change. When a proactive law centre identifies a particular local group or a neighbourhood as a community – or conceives of it as such – it does not automatically assume that the members of the group or neighbourhood enjoy a pervasive and interlocking set of affective, mutually satisfying, and face – to – face relationships. A sense of personal belonging *may* exist, but its absence need not necessarily deter the law centre's community worker, for the community worker may be able to help create such a sense as the group or neighbourhood works together to pursue strategies designed to ameliorate problems that its members experience in common. Many tenants' associations have benefited from the existence of affective, face – to – face relationships within the group, but the prime motivating force behind the creation of such associations has often been the experience of poor housing, which is shared by the members. Groups such as tenants' associations may also be seen as potential vehicles for limited social change both in terms of improving the housing conditions of their members and of developing their social skills and competences.

Agencies such as NNLC attempt to form individuals with a common problem or experience into organized groups, so that they can be encouraged to articulate their grievances and to seek collective solutions. In this sense, the concepts of community adopted by NNLC are closely associated with the idea of the group as both a target for organization and a vehicle for social change. This targeting effort takes place within the wider context of a physical locality that the law centre's staff have identified through long and close involvement in the area. NNLC has, in effect, defined a particular geographical locality as a 'community' suffering from serious housing problems.

The concepts of community employed by NNLC, whether they refer to target groups, vehicles for social change, or actual locality, are all *sensitizing and organizing principles*. They help the staff of the law centre to focus on certain social relationships and phenomena relevant to particular issues and to exclude others, thereby creating a necessary boundary to subsequent analysis and action. NNLC staff have argued that by virtue of their personal involvement in the locality, they are acquainted with many of the physical, political, economic, and environmental characteristics of the centre's catchment area. In their view this allows them to identify possible issues of common concern, and to draw on relevant local knowledge when considering collective strategies to address those concerns. NNLC attempts to foster a sense of common endeavour among the groups with which it comes into contact; and it tries to encourage group members to become actively involved in the running of the groups. In this way NNLC is seeking to create a sense of personal belonging among group members and to develop their skills and competences. This is the final sense in which NNLC would speak of community – affective, face – to – face relationships among group members.

The Nature of Community Action

There is no single method of community intervention, although Rothman has identified three variants. The first model or variant, locality development, pursues broad social change in an area on the basis of general participation by the inhabitants of that area in the formulation of the goals and activities connected with the proposed social change (Rothman, 1968:19). The second model, social planning, emphasizes the technical nature of solving social problems and depends to a large extent on the role of expert planners. The task is essentially one of how best to deliver goods and services to a target population; the social planning approach is not concerned with building community capacity (Rothman, 1968:20). Whereas the law centre movement as whole would agree with the sentiments expressed in the first model, law centres are antagonistic towards the social planning model since it is no part of their role to limit in any way the participation of clients in those decisions that affect their own lives. The social planning approach tends to do just this. It undervalues the contributions of lay people precisely because it is a model of action heavily influenced by the views of the 'expert' planners.

The model of community intervention, which most closely accords with the operational philosophy of proactive law centres, is Rothman's third variant.

> ...the social action approach presupposes a disadvantaged segment of the population that needs to be organised, perhaps in alliance with others, in order to make adequate demands on the larger community for increased resources or treatment more in accordance with social justice or democracy. It aims at making basic changes in major institutions or community practices. Social action as employed here seeks redistribution of power, resources, or decision – making in the community and/or changing basic policies of formal organizations (Rothman, 1968:20 – 1).

This model also brings to mind aspects of Galanter's ideas on access to legality and how securing the various benefits of legality need not be attempted through the use of legal strategies alone. The focus by proactive law centres on encouraging client groups to become involved in local decision – making forums is both an example of a non – legal strategy and a route through which access to legality and some of the rights of citizenship may be secured.

Knowledge about the Community

No matter which of the three approaches to community intervention is adopted, each practitioner relies heavily on the depth and quality of knowledge about the community that he or she can gather. As Kramer and Specht (1975:9) have argued: 'each practitioner requires the same kinds of knowledge to carry out the tasks involved in his work. Each faces, however, distinctive dilemmas'. For example, local authority planning and housing departments require information in relation to housing needs, state of housing repair, special requirements of various groups within the local population, etc., before they can carry out proposed housing rehabilitation and redevelopment schemes. Whereas these departments may at times find this kind of information difficult to come by, it is the same information that proactive law centres more easily gather as they seek to encourage tenant groups to become involved in the decision – making processes related to such schemes.

Whenever proactive law centres have been working with local groups in respect of housing schemes, they have usually found that any strategy adopted to represent the interests of the groups has depended on the relevant information about housing needs, etc., being made freely available by the residents and tenants involved. Knowledge about the community and the needs and problems of its people is of vital importance to practitioners, not only for the identification of relevant issues, but also for the manner in which solutions to common problems are pursued. This information, held by the practitioner in conjunction with expertise about legal and non – legal strategies, facilitates his twin roles as enabler and organizer. In practice the roles overlap. While an organizer may have to follow a somewhat directive approach, at least initially, in order to get a group successfully off the ground, nevertheless as an enabler the practitioner is essentially interested in stimulating 'the group to make its own decisions and to assume maximum responsibility for the implementation of these decisions' (Spergel, 1975:315).

In other words, group organization may initially be stimulated by the activities of community work practitioners. This may mean that the practitioner surveys a particular street or area with a view to uncovering the extent of housing problems. Then he may try to persuade the inhabitants, through the distribution of leaflets and the holding of public meetings, to form a tenants' association to counter these problems. However, in order to act as an enabler a more non – directive approach must be adopted. It is precisely this approach, though not referred to as such, that NNLC has embraced.

In order for a primarily non – directive approach to operate successfully certain conditions must usually be present, which provide the potential for community groups to act in a self – directed manner. Batten (1975:12 – 13) described these conditions as follows:

1. that a number of people are dissatisfied with things as they are, and are agreed on something which they all feel as a specific want;
2. that they realise that this want is likely to remain unmet unless they do something about it themselves;
3. that they have, or have access to, sufficient resources to be able to achieve what they want to achieve. This implies that they have (or can get):
(a) enough knowledge to enable them to make a wise decision about what they want to do and how best to do it;
(b) enough resources of knowledge, skill, and equipment actually to do it; and
(c) a sufficiently strong incentive to keep them together while they carry the project through.
If the want is strong enough, and the other conditions are all present, then people will act without outside help. Unfortunately, more often than not they are not all present. This is why many potentially valuable need – meeting autonomous groups either do not form, or if they do form, quickly die: and this is why community workers, if they wish, can find ample scope for using the non – directive approach.
The non – directive approach, therefore, is the method adopted by an enabler who is trying to encourage the development among group

members of self – direction and self – help. To achieve this end the enabler must fulfil four goals.

First, the enabler must encourage group members to articulate their own demands and to focus on issues of common concern. Second, he must provide information about how similar groups have acted in the past, including information about how they have chosen to organize themselves. Third, the enabler must help people to think critically about what difficulties might be encountered as the group tries to seek solutions to collective problems, and how best to overcome these problems. Finally, the enabler must suggest sources from which the group can obtain technical and other assistance in addition to what it provides for itself (Batten, 1975:13 – 14).

The concepts of informed consent and of people – working are crucial in any realization of these four goals within the non – directive approach. At NNLC the adoption of a primarily non – directive style is intended to make the best use of scarce resources, to encourage the emergence of new skills and competences among group members, to promote social solidarity within groups, and to provide opportunities for group members to think critically about the problems they face. Let me now turn to a detailed treatment of the work of NNLC so that the centre's use of the non – directive approach and its deployment of other proactive concepts, such as people – working and informed consent, can be evaluated.

The Northern Neighbourhood Law Centre: A Case – Study

The Origins and Goals of NNLC

The proactive emphasis of NNLC is rooted in its origins. The centre began its work in 1971 in response to a demand from local tenants' groups for a legal advice service that could function as a basic resource to community organizations. With a small amount of charitable funds the centre operated a weekly evening advice service from the premises of a local church. The two community workers operating the service had previously been involved in the affairs of several of the tenants' groups, and they brought to the advice sessions specialist knowledge in housing law. Six volunteer private solicitors were also involved in running the advice sessions. Shortly after beginning the advice service, NNLC moved into permanent offices at an unobtrusive location. It also became a registered charity, and during the period of my research on the centre it remained wholly funded by various charities. However, these funds were never extensive and, consequently, NNLC has always existed as a small – scale operation. Indeed, in order to supplement their own salaries, and in keeping with their philosophy of self – help, the members of staff worked from time to time on a number of community projects in the area.

84

As the pressure of work grew – the centre acted more and more as a resource for local groups and left the evening advice sessions increasingly to volunteer staff – a barrister was taken on in 1973, and in 1976 another community worker joined the team of four staff. The first three members of staff had all lived and worked in the law centre's catchment area for several years prior to the formation of NNLC, and they had all been involved in local affairs through their membership of tenants' associations and participation in local campaigns and issues.

One of the centre's primary goals was to encourage the formation of self – reliant organized groups, which would not become dependent upon the knowledge and skills of professionals. This focus on groupwork sprang not only from the centre's original association with existing local groups, but also from the beliefs of the staff who felt that a collective approach offered greater scope in tackling housing problems than working with individual clients. They also argued that working with groups provided 'the opportunity to encourage ordinary people to reflect about their problems in a critical and creative way...' (NNLC, 1975 – 7:15). NNLC staff wanted to forge a participatory relationship with their client groups by ensuring the operation of high levels of informed consent and of people – working techniques. However, they were conscious of the fact that the law centre should not act as 'a mechanism for creating grievances, but [as] a vehicle for their articulation (Adamsdown Community Trust, 1978:63). To this end, NNLC tried to

> work *with* people rather than *for* them. This has meant that wherever possible we have brought people with similar problems together so that they can tackle their problems collectively. In doing so, they learn how to cope with different establishment bodies, such as the Council, courts of policy. More important they realise they can exercise control over their own lives (NNLC, 1974:2, Original italics).

The aim of this approach was to foster self – reliance among group members, and in order to do so the centre adopted a low – profile style in which members would not feel intimidated by an image of traditional professionalism. Indeed, NNLC staff were trying to promote a new kind of professionalism; one in which professional expertise was shared with group members, and in which the professional encouraged the group members to use that expertise themselves as part of a self – help outcome. This form of professionalism owes much to Bennett and Hokenstad's concept of people – working. As such, the law centre recognized not only the expertise of its own staff members, but also the different areas of expertise and of information that would be held by the groups themselves. Within this participatory framework NNLC attempted to encourage the development of active client groups, which would become involved in those decision – making processes affecting their own lives. In summary, a major goal of NNLC was to identify and encourage the capacity of client groups to become self – reliant, and to increase that capacity through the development of client competence and party upgrading. The fulfilment of such a goal called for the active involvement of clients rather than their passive compliance with whatever had been decided by professionals as being the best course of action.

Work with Individuals

As one would expect with a closed – door agency the level of individual casework conducted at NNLC was much smaller than that at an open – door reactive law centre. As a result of the centre's unobtrusive and unpublicized location, the majority of individuals who came into contact with the centre did so during one of its evening advice sessions held at a local church. These sessions were coordinated by the full – time law centre staff but actually conducted by volunteer solicitors and community workers. During these sessions each client discusses various courses of action available to solve his problem. Moreover:

> the Law Centre prefers to act in a supportive role, going with a person to the Rent Tribunal or the court and writing letters on their behalf where necessary. One of the [volunteers] will follow up the case until it has been satisfactorily dealt with, but strong emphasis is placed on building up the individual's confidence and self reliance (NNLC, 1974:1).

However, the volunteers also referred clients to private solicitors if they had problems that could not be handled on the basis of a weekly advice session. No proper check was made to see if clients actually went to meet the solicitors to whom they had been referred. Obviously, when clients are sent elsewhere then the law centre can make no claim at all that their self – reliance and competence are being developed. Nevertheless, the evening advice sessions arguably fulfilled a more important function for clients than that of fostering self – reliance; and that was simply to provide assistance for those who were experiencing problems that could not be grouped with others similarly placed and pursued in a collective fashion. The evening advice sessions were, therefore, a useful mechanism for servicing individual cases without drawing upon a significant part of the time and resources of the law centre's full – time staff.

Moreover, the adoption of evening advice sessions to provide a service for individuals with problems not suitable for a collective approach also helped to solve a professional and ethical dilemma facing NNLC's staff. Put starkly that dilemma was deciding what to do, in the context of a closed – door, group – oriented law centre, with individual clients. The advice sessions staffed by volunteers was NNLC's answer. Despite the fact that NNLC wanted to adopt the same aims of encouraging self – reliance and developing client competence whether working with groups or individuals, one cannot assume that these aims were necessarily fulfilled. Encouraging self – reliance in a group context is a very different phenomenon from confronting individuals of low socio – economic status with a self – help option that may appear to them to be unreasonable and even onerous.

Work with Groups

Given my particular interest in the way in which law centres approached housing problems, I decided to focus my attention on the work that NNLC had conducted with a number of tenants' groups within its catchment area[7]. Four such groups were analysed in detail, and all of them were groups where NNLC had been responsible for the initial organizational stimuli. My intention was not only to understand the manner in which NNLC worked with local groups, but also to evaluate as far as possible the extent to which the relationship between NNLC and tenants' groups led to the realization of various proactive concepts, such as informed consent, people – working techniques, client competence, communal control, party upgrading, and client participation. The four groups, to which I have given fictitious names, were the Feering Street Tenants' Association, Wharf Mews Tenants' Association, Witham Street Tenants' Association, and Stone – Blackwood Tenants' Cooperative. Fictitious titles are also given to the names of property companies and other organizations that figure in the following accounts of the four tenants' groups[8].

Feering Street Tenants' Association: Rogerton, a property company that owned most of the houses in Feering Street, had been trying for some years to gain vacant possession of its tenanted dwellings so that they could be renovated and then sold off to owner occupiers. In 1971 there remained a hard core of tenants who had refused all offers to vacate their homes. A campaign of harassment was allegedly begun by Rogerton towards the end of 1972, and resulted in 1973 in a meeting between NNLC staff and some of the tenants of the street who had become increasingly worried by the company's behaviour, and also by the actions of Granley, another property company to which Rogerton had sold some of its houses.

As a result of this meeting NNLC arranged to talk to all of the tenants in the street who expressed great dissatisfaction with their landlords. It was decided at a further meeting of the tenants to petition the local council and, following legal advice from NNLC about the poor state of repair of many of the tenancies, the meeting also decided to approach public health inspectors to survey the disrepaired homes owned by the two property companies. The lack of an adequate response from these quarters led in March 1973 to a meeting between thirteen Feering Street tenants, some local councillors, and NNLC staff. NNLC staff outlined a number of options for dealing with the problems of harassment and disrepair, and the pros and cons of each were discussed in the meeting. The tenants themselves eventually decided that the option they preferred was the compulsory purchase of their homes, a course of action subsequently agreed to by the council.

In order to help the council in the preparation of the compulsory purchase orders (CPOs) the tenants agreed to supply information about the extent and nature of the disrepair in Feering Street. The tenants were advised about what information to collect by NNLC. The survey undertaken by the tenants revealed that there were thirty three remaining tenants, eleven houses were in need of urgent repair and that all of the houses (twenty four in total) were in poor condition, sixty five rooms were empty, and only five houses were still fully tenanted. As a result of the experience of conducting the survey, the tenants decided in May 1973 to constitute themselves formally as a tenants' association and to elect a chairman and committee.

The association's first decision was to press more strongly for the CPOs by publicizing its case in a local newspaper in an attempt to keep the pressure on the local council to speed up its commitment to compulsory purchase. At the end of July the council did resolve to make CPOs on twenty one houses in the street. In September and October, under the threat of compulsory purchase, both property companies sold their houses to the council. It was at this stage that NNLC ceased to be actively involved in the work of the association. However, the group continued to operate for the tenants took the view that while they had won the first part of their struggle – to have their homes taken into council ownership – they had not yet been victorious in the second part; namely, to have their homes properly repaired and renovated.

Accordingly, the association was involved in a series of meetings with the council's housing department, which led to the creation of a joint consultation system. This meant that the association provided the housing department with a list of those families who wanted to find alternative accommodation quickly, and those who wished to remain in the street in the renovated houses. For those who opted for alternative accommodation the association negotiated their right to return to the renovated properties, if they wished, when the repair work was finished. For its part, the housing department agreed to submit detailed plans for the renovation of the street to the association. It found the first plan unacceptable and a second incorporated many of the suggestions made by the association. However, it was only at the third attempt that the housing department's renovation scheme met with the full approval of the tenants, the very people whose lives would be most affected by the plan.

The association's sense of determination and solidarity were important factors in its attempts to influence the decision–making processes that would affect the lives of its members. The struggle concerning alleged property speculation and the subsequent issue of the renovation of the houses were carried on by a cohesive organization whose members enjoyed high levels of face–to–face interaction. The tenants' association was an extension of the sense of community that already existed within Feering Street. Later I shall consider to what extent its members actually experienced and developed the various concepts associated with the proactive approach.

Wharf Mews Tenants' Association: The association was composed of approximately two hundred families living on a newly built estate owned by the Wharf Housing Association and managed by a housing trust. NNLC's involvement began in 1974 when many of the residents, who had been nominated for tenancies by the local council as a result of their previous poor housing conditions, were confused and anxious about the terms of their leases. Some of the residents assumed that their landlord was the housing trust to which they paid rent, and others disliked some of the conditions attached to the lease, such as the stipulation that the residents had to pay for communal lighting on the estate and for repairs to the central heating system if it broke down. Moreover, there were a number of other petty restrictions to which many tenants objected.

NNLC arranged a meeting for the tenants to discuss these and other issues. It emerged that there was also widespread dissatisfaction with the housing trust and its style of estate management, which was viewed as impersonal and inflexible. During the meeting, at the suggestion of NNLC, the estate's residents agreed to constitute themselves formally as a tenants' association and a chairman and committee were elected. The association's first decision was to seek renegotiation of the tenancy agreements, and on the advice of NNLC it was decided to bypass the housing trust and to negotiate directly with the Wharf Housing Association about the adoption of a new lease. During these negotiations NNLC staff advised the tenants' association on important legal aspects of tenancy agreements and they were also able to provide examples of appropriate wording for parts of the lease so that the new agreement fully reflected the wishes of the association's members. A new agreement was finally signed that gave the tenants the same rights of security as those in the private sector.

Following the successful renegotiation of the lease the association went on to develop a range of other activities without any further assistance from NNLC. These activities were designed to promote the well–being of the estate's residents and included in 1975 the setting up of a small community centre, the organization of social events such as raffles and barbecues, and the creation of children's play facilities and a youth club. Later in the year the association entered into discussions with the local authority for the building of a five–a–side football pitch on the estate.

In subsequent meetings with the housing association, the tenants succeeded in having the housing trust removed from the management of the estate. Instead, the housing association decided to appoint its own management officer, and the tenants' association itself took an active role in his selection.

Further dealings with the Wharf Housing Association led to the appointment of two tenant representatives on the Association's board. Regular monthly consultative meetings between the two organizations led to a swifter conclusion of the repairs being carried out on the estate, which had been necessitated by the incomplete and occasionally sub – standard nature of the building work. These meetings also initiated a better method of refuse collection and the installation of a more satisfactory heating system in many of the flats.

In all of the association's work a major theme has been the need to maintain high levels of face – to – face interaction among as many of the estate's residents as possible. The association's members looked on their organization not only as a way of protecting their interests as tenants, but also as a means of developing a sense of community among the people of a newly built and settled estate.

Witham Street Tenants' Association: Personal contact and knowledge of the area first drew to the attention of NNLC staff in 1973 the emergence of a housing problem in and around Witham Street. A survey conducted by the law centre revealed a growing number of incidences of houses in disrepair, of harassment, and of illegal eviction. NNLC organized a small number of the affected tenants into a group in the hope that other similarly affected individuals would also join. The law centre noted that in any attempt to organize local people into a coherent group 'the drive for organisation must come from within' (NNLC, 1974:11). When, a short while later, the threat of eviction passed away that drive for organization was no longer apparent, and the original group of tenants ceased to exist.

However, throughout 1974 the standards of repair in the majority of houses in and around Witham Street worsened, which prompted the local council in January 1975 to seek CPOs on most of the properties. At this point NNLC reappeared on the scene to explain to tenants the possible outcomes of CPOs being made on their homes. Also at this stage, it became clear that there was a much greater drive for organization among the tenants as they came to realize the implications of the council's decision. The Witham Street Tenants' Association was formed in April 1975 at a public meeting organized by NNLC. The first and most major decision facing its members was whether to press the council to rehabilitate their homes, or to support a scheme for the redevelopment of the area. An overwhelming majority preferred renovation to the bulldozer. A few meetings later the association decided to produce a monthly newsletter and to create a system of street representatives whose role it was to contact tenants and to gather any information from them that might be required. These elected representatives also acted as a link between the association's general committee and the membership, and they were able to keep everybody informed of developments.

Before the council made much progress on the CPOs, the area was declared in July 1975 an Housing Action Area (HAA) in which the Witham Street group was the only organized tenants' group in the locality. NNLC sought the help of the association in canvassing the rest of the HAA and in encouraging other tenants to form organized groups. As a result of these combined efforts two new groups were set up in the area. At around the same time, the Witham Street association was conducting an intensive survey of the state of disrepair and lack of amenities in many of its members' houses, and of the rehabilitation preferences of its members. The completion of the survey not only tested the commitment and competence of the group, but also opened up an important channel of communication between itself and the council. The survey information gathered by the association and passed on to the council proved to be most valuable, for as the council itself acknowledged:

> Information subsequently obtained from the Witham Street Tenants' Association indicated that the majority of tenants wished to remain in Witham Street and that there is a larger proportion of one and two person households. The rehabilitation scheme originally prepared for the Compulsory Purchase Order feasibility study provided mainly 4 and 6 person dwellings and is therefore not suited to the needs of the existing tenants.

Statements such as this alerted the association to the importance of becoming involved in joint consultation with the council concerning the rehabilitation of the street. Indeed, there was a need to extend the consultation process throughout the whole of the HAA and , accordingly, the council set up a sub–committee of the housing committee to discuss plans for the area. The Witham Street group 'fought to have representation in proportion to their numbers in the area on this committee' (NNLC, 1975–7:5), and succeeded in securing two such representatives.

In February 1976 when the CPOs were discussed at a public enquiry the association presented a detailed case supporting the council's decision to seek compulsory purchase. The strength of the association's case rested on the information gathered from the detailed survey of the street. Each tenant had completed a questionnaire asking for information on the following: rent levels, number and description of rooms and amenities, incidences of non–repair or harassment by landlords, evidence of adjacent vacant tenancies, number of persons living in each tenancy, etc. An account was then prepared for each house in the street setting out the number of tenancies, whether the landlord was resident or non–resident, a statement of the size of each tenancy, and a description of the lack of basic amenities, disrepair, or other relevant factors. The worst houses were written up as case–studies highlighting the deprivations experienced by the more unfortunate tenants.

The association had been advised by NNLC on the sorts of information the survey should seek to uncover, but it was the members of the group who had been responsible for carrying out the survey, organizing its findings, and presenting them to the public enquiry. From reading copies of the association's monthly newsletter, it was also clear to me that some of the members, at least, had gained a detailed understanding of the process of seeking CPOs.

The CPOs were confirmed in November 1976 but virtually no repair work was undertaken by the council in the months that followed. Many of the association's members were angry by this lack of progress and, following information received from NNLC, the group decided early in 1977 to threaten the council with a summons under section 99 of the 1936 Public Health Act in respect of a few houses where conditions of disrepair had significantly worsened. Repairs to these properties were soon set in motion and in the end the summons was not issued. The association continued to meet regularly to try to ensure that repairs were carried out as promptly as possible and in accordance with the needs and wishes of the tenants.

Stone – Blackwood Tenants' Cooperative: This group was established in October 1975 as a result of negotiations between NNLC, the council, and Marksfield Housing Association. The idea of a cooperative came from NNLC's involvement with a playgroup in Stone ward where some of the mothers reported poor housing conditions as tenants in the private sector and little prospect of improvement. The first twelve members of the cooperative were drawn from among those families whose children attended this playgroup and subsequent members came from the nearby Blackwood ward. By March 1976 there were thirty five members and, until the cooperative knew how many houses it would receive from the Marksfield Housing Association, it was decided to halt further recruitment. In January 1976, the group had organized itself formally with the election of a chairman and committee and the holding of fortnightly general meetings. Immediately the cooperative began to gather information and to develop plans concerning the supervision and control of the properties it was to be allocated. Part of these plans was the creation of an allocation committee whose role it was to make recommendations about which families were to be allocated tenancies in the first batch of houses from the housing association. By June 1976 the cooperative felt able to state in one of its internal documents that 'it had convinced the local council and the housing association that 'the co – op was now capable of taking on the management of dwellings and that it would allocate the flats on a fair and proper basis'.

NNLC staff had been involved with the cooperative until June 1976, advising on organizational structure and the procedure for the cooperative to register as a housing association in its own right. After that time the cooperative ran off its own steam, which meant large attendances at general meetings and a strong common commitment to achieve a clearly formulated goal; namely, to move into decent and acceptable accommodation. All of the members had a common background of living in poor housing conditions and all shared the hope that the cooperative would prove the most effective way of leaving those conditions behind. For the majority, who also wanted to remain living in the same area, the cooperative offered its members the opportunity for continuity of children's schooling and of local friendships and attachments. This common experience and purpose, and the strong face – to – face relationships built up within the cooperative, were much valued by members. Accordingly, they were anxious that the group should not become too large and impersonal.

The social solidarity and cohesion of the cooperative had been an important factor in overcoming the potentially disruptive effects of the allocation of the first batch of nine houses handed over by the housing association in July 1976. The elected members of the allocation committee had selected tenants for these dwellings in keeping with a dual determination of the housing needs of particular members, and the amount of time and effort each one had devoted to the cooperative. In discharging this role the cooperative's members felt that the allocation committee had acted more efficiently and humanely than the council's housing department could have done. They reasoned that the committee was much better placed than any official of the housing department to gather appropriate information about housing need and to distinguish more sensitively between the competing needs of individual members. Thus, while the allocation did not pass without some disagreement, it did not lead to the disruption of the work of the cooperative nor did it damage general social relations among the members. The allocation of the second batch of houses a few months later passed off with even less disagreement than before, which testified to the open and effective manner in which the process of allocation was approached.

In the wake of the then allocation of twenty tenancies two members in possession of allocated dwellings ceased to attend general meetings. The rest of the cooperative's members, however, insisted that this was the exception to the rule, and they described various ways in which the cooperative hoped to encourage the continued participation of everyone. For example, all of the cooperative's tenants were involved in a scheme for reporting and carrying out repairs; all tenants paid their rents in the first instance into the cooperative's own bank account; and most of the cooperative's members – whether selected for a tenancy or not – were involved in discussions to find ways of exercising more control over the properties allocated to them. This desire for greater control eventually led to the cooperative registering with the Housing Corporation as a cooperative housing association in its own right.

Following registration the cooperative was allocated a further twenty dwellings to be owned and developed by the cooperative itself. With forty properties in all for which the cooperative had some responsibility, towards the end of 1976 the cooperative began to discuss how it could ensure the continued involvement of its members within a highly personalized face – to – face approach. This sense of personal involvement and the cooperative's ability to respond to individual needs were important factors in the continuation of its work. Indeed, spurred on by confidence in its achievements, the cooperative also looked into the feasibility of plans for a food cooperative and a day nursery. According to NNLC the work of the cooperative has provided the opportunity for its members 'to gain confidence and to set up a structure that allows them to collectively own and manage their own improved housing' (NNLC, 1975 – 7:5).

NNLC And Citizenship: An Evaluation Of Proactivity

The proactive delivery of legal and non – legal services is an alternative to that of the reactive delivery system. Having provided four case – studies of NNLC's involvement with local groups, I can now comment on the centre's proactive orientation, its consequences for clients, the processes it adopted, and how these processes fared in the wider socio – economic context in which NNLC operated.

One of the difficulties with the proactive approach, as with community work in general, is that it is an approach that is more diffuse, more uncertain, and potentially more wide – ranging than other more circumscribed methods of intervention and representation. Accordingly, one must be careful not to generalize too far on the basis of the proactive activities conducted at NNLC. Much of the wider literature on proactivity and the actual evidence from a variety of community work projects can serve only as general signposts in this evaluation – they are not precise points of reference but rather they constitute a benchmark against which to locate the particular operations of NNLC. The *specific* processes and concepts that NNLC sought to implement through its operations were informed consent, people – working techniques, client competence, party upgrading, communal control, and client participation. These are the precise goals that NNLC set for itself and I shall be evaluating the extent to which NNLC was able to realize them operationally in a short while.

There were also more *general* processes taking place at the centre, which constitute a wider context in the evaluation of the work of NNLC. These general processes included the use of sensitizing and organizing principles relevant to community work practice; the attempt to identify target groups as vehicles for limited social change; and the deployment of 'political' strategies to achieve collective goals.

Some General Issues

As Batten (1975:12 – 14) has pointed out, an agency such as NNLC that wishes to adopt a low – profile, non – directive approach must be aware of those conditions favourable and unfavourable to the success

94

of proactive involvement in organized groups. By virtue of the extensive range of personal contacts in the locality enjoyed by NNLC staff, the centre has usually been able to judge correctly when and where most of the favourable conditions were present. Although it has not been infallible in its judgement, as the later examples of Ashby Square and Mentley Avenue tenants' associations will show, the law centre enjoyed considerable success with the groups described in the four case – studies. In each case the centre realized that there were a number of people dissatisfied with some aspect of their housing status and who were prepared to try to do something about it. Moreover, NNLC supplied sufficient resources of skill, expertise, and initial organizing impetus to demonstrate to each group the potential ways in which its housing situation could be improved. Furthermore, each group enjoyed sufficient incentive among its membership to keep together as an organized entity while pursuing collective solutions for its grievances. In this respect, NNLC was successful in identifying appropriate target groups and in organizing them into coherent bodies with a common grievance and goal. Whether these groups succeeded in acting as vehicles for limited social change will be discussed later. However, some of the other consequences of this targeting can be aired now.

Given the predominant group focus of the centre, NNLC's style of intervention in the community had little relevance for the problems of individuals *qua* individuals. In the main, an individual's housing problem was only handled if that person was a part of an original target group identified by NNLC, or subsequently became a member of such a group. In this sense the decision to pursue *collective* solutions and to combine legal and non – legal strategies had already been made by NNLC. This raises not only the issue of communal control – a topic for consideration towards the end of the chapter – but also the *political* nature of proactive intervention.

It can be argued that the kind of intervention practised by NNLC is 'political', and that it is therefore not proper for a law centre to pursue such activities. There are a number of views to consider here. The Law Centres' Working Group, as it was then called, argued that:

> With limited resources, it is more effective to concentrate on the source of a problem rather than to attempt to alleviate its effect by legal action in individual cases. Accordingly, some law centres have assisted groups campaigning against bad housing, unemployment and other problems, sometimes by direct participation, sometimes, quite properly, by giving legal advice (Royal Commission on Legal Services, 1979:80, para 8.8).

The Royal Commission on Legal Services (RCLS), however, maintained that such campaigns have sometimes been controversial and have prompted some funding bodies to threaten to cut off their financial backing for the law centres concerned. It proposed, therefore, that a law centre should not carry out general community work in the kind of manner adopted at NNLC; that is to say, no law centre should organize groups to bring pressure on landlords, nor should it urge changes in priorities for public expenditure (RCLS, 1979:83 – 4, paras 8.19 – 8.20). The Commission had no objection to law centres providing legal advice and assistance to existing groups, but it held to the view that no law centre should 'devote its resources to taking part in political or community activities...' (RCLS, 1979:84, para, 8.21). By taking part in such acts the Commission felt that law centres would be overstepping their function, which was to provide *legal* advice to their clientele. Moreover, in the Commission's view, community action would involve a law centre with particular sections of its community rather than being a service freely available to all. Finally, it was argued that involvement in campaigns would undermine the ability of law centres to provide an independent service (RCLS, 1979:83 – 4, para, 8.20).

The thrust of the criticisms voiced by the Royal Commission centred on the work of some law centres in organizing individuals into groups and then employing legal and non – legal strategies to mount campaigns, to pressurize local councils, and to engage in what the Commission perceived as political activities. Clearly, the work of NNLC and of some other proactive law centres would not have met with the Commission's approval. However, a defence to the criticisms of the Commission can be made, which goes beyond the rather general justification for a group focus put forward by the Law Centres' Working Group, (subsequently the Law Centres' Federation).

The Commission was clearly correct when it raised no objections to law centres giving legal advice and assistance to existing local groups. The political dimensions of the work of law centres to which the Commission objected were not therefore connected with the actual giving of legal advice to groups but with the nature of other aspects of the relationship between those groups and law centres. The Commission was concerned about the following kinds of questions. Is it acceptable for law centres actually to organize local groups? Which groups will be selected? Which issues will be pursued? They raise important issues to explore in defending law centres against the charge of political involvement.

Concerning the questions of which groups will be selected and which issues will be pursued, there is obviously great scope within most communities to create groups and to address issues across a wide range. Proactive law centres in general, however, and NNLC in particular, have concentrated on groups that have problems amenable to solutions, either wholly or in part, through the use of legal avenues. The legal dimension, therefore, in the selection of groups to organize and of issues to pursue has been of primary importance. In fact, proactive law centres working with groups have been no different in this respect from reactive centres, for both kinds of law centre have addressed problems that potentially have a legal solution. Proactive centres have differed from reactive agencies in seeking solutions via a combination of legal and *non – legal* tactics.

Even so, the focus on the legal dimension is one part of the defence against the charge that proactive law centres are too political. The pursuit of legal rights is a freedom open to us all, and it can hardly be said (in a pejorative way) that the legitimate pursuit of clients' rights constitutes an unacceptably political dimension to the work of proactive law centres.

The other part of the defence must address the question about whether law centres should become involved in the actual organizing of groups, which seems to me to be the aspect of the proactive approach that most critics refer to as the clearest example of acting in a 'political' manner. Law centres have a mandate to provide legal assistance, but do they have one to intervene in the community by organizing individuals into coherent groups? Those who argue that law centres have no mandate for this latter aspect are worried that such groups and their constituent members may become dominated by activist, articulate lawyers and community workers. One response to these worries is to argue that proactive law centres encourage their clients to run their own groups and to take responsibility for pursuing collective forms of action. Whether professional intervention in these groups leads to domination depends on the levels of informed consent, people – working, and client competence that law centre staff can develop in their clients. The four NNLC case – studies provide sufficient information to suggest that NNLC staff did not dominate the goals and activities of the community groups. Indeed, there is evidence to show the emergence of indigenous leadership and of client competence as group members took on the responsibilities of the day – to – day functioning of their respective organizations. But if the charge of domination now appears to be overstating the danger, can proactive law centres be defended on the charge of manipulation?

According to the Law Centres' Federation (1977:3), groupwork
is the development of communal self – help facilities: it is the exploitation of test cases (in a wide sense); it is work which links the general with the particular – the community with the individual; work which encourages communal responsibility and discourages dependency.

An empirical study by Adamsdown Law Centre delved into the nature of groupwork to discover whether it could give rise to dependency, and whether it could lead to domination of people so that they became cajoled into taking action with which they disagreed. Adamsdown reported that:
There is no doubt that there have been occasions where [law centre] staff have suggested issues to management committees as matters of concern – perhaps because there appear to be legal possibilities – but where in the event the issue fails for lack of a constituency. And if there is no constituency, it will always fail. In deprived communities there are so many issues potentially to take up that only those which touch a nerve of genuine concern can have any hope of a successful candidature for

Law Centre resources (Adamsdown Community Trust, 1978:61). The terms 'constituency' and 'nerve of concern', like NNLC's reference to the 'drive for organisation from within', all reflect the wishes and demands of clients. Where this constituency, concern, or drive are absent groups do not form and persist. Where they are present, where people have a problem in common, and where they want to do something about it – then, and only then, is there a basis for group formation and continuation. The evidence suggests that proactive law centres articulate existing grievances; they do not create them. In this way, there is little substance to the charge that proactive law centres manipulate clients.

The debate about the real or imagined political dimensions of the work of proactive law centres persists. In the end it is the perceptions held by funding agencies about the political dimensions of proactivity that are likely to have the biggest outcome on this debate. For if the funders decide that proactive law centres are too political or too controversial – whatever it is they understand by these terms – then they are unlikely either to continue existing funding or to make available extra funds for the creation of new proactive centres.

The issues of funding and of the impact of proactive law centres will be subjects in the final chapter. Now I propose to turn to the specific goals and processes adopted by NNLC; namely, informed consent, people – working, client competence, communal control, party upgrading, and client participation. I shall be evaluating the extent to which NNLC has been able to realize them in its work with local groups.

Informed Consent

Informed consent is the process by which professional practitioners set out possible ways to proceed and explain to clients the merits and demerits of each. Each option, assuming there is more than one, should be explored jointly by professional and client, and it should be the client who takes responsibility for the final selection. Such a process can apply to legal and non – legal courses of action and, as Rosenthal has already indicated, informed consent may actually increase the efficiency and productivity of representation.

The process of informed consent can be seen at work in the operation of NNLC. For example, NNLC advised the Feering Street Tenants' Association on the possibilities of presenting a petition to the local council about the issues of harassment and disrepair. At later meetings of the association NNLC offered advice on the role of public health legislation in trying to combat disrepair. The Feering Street group decided to pursue action on both of these fronts. It also decided that it would press for compulsory purchase orders on the dwellings of its members and that it would undertake a survey of the extent of disrepair. The Witham Street Tenants' Association decided to pursue this same course . In the latter case

NNLC explained to the Witham Street group what the council's decision to seek CPOs on their properties might mean in terms of rehabilitation of its members' homes or redevelopment. Both associations not only preferred compulsory purchase but also were strongly in favour of the dwellings being renovated in ways that satisfied the housing needs of their respective members. Both groups opted to conduct a survey of the dwellings and were advised by NNLC about the information the surveys should gather.

In the case of the Witham Street association its members opted for a system of street representatives and took further advice from NNLC on the use of public health legislation as a means of speeding up repairs to the properties. The association also asked for advice from NNLC about taking one of the few remaining private landlords in the street to the Rent Tribunal in order to secure rent reductions. All of these decisions were the product of discussions at general meetings of the respective associations. Although most of these options came originally from NNLC staff, it was the membership that took responsibility for implementing these options. This is hardly surprising when so many of the options require decisions of principle to be made by those who will be affected by those decisions; such as whether to seek redress for disrepair by pursuing private landlords through the courts or to press for CPOs, or whether to opt for the renovation of one's current accommodation or to seek redevelopment and alternative accommodation elsewhere.

At Wharf Mews Tenants' Association the main issue of informed consent concerned the renegotiation of the tenancy agreement and the decision to do this directly with the housing association rather than with its management team. At Stone – Blackwood Tenants' Cooperative the main issues to be decided were the structure and running of the cooperative and the allocation of properties. The cooperative's members opted for an open and democratic structure with an elected allocation committee to ensure an equitable distribution of dwellings. Part of the allocation process was the survey conducted by the cooperative into the housing needs of its members. A while later NNLC advised the cooperative about how to become registered in its own right as a cooperative housing association, which was in response to the members' preferences to exercise more control over their own dwellings.

In these various ways informed consent was a process that not only encouraged clients to become actively involved in the running of their respective groups, but also helped to foster membership solidarity and cohesion. These two factors were important characteristics of all four case – studies, and it would appear that without them groups are unlikely to exist for any length of time.

People – Working

This is a process in which information is imparted to clients about their position, and the insights and expertise of professionals are shared with them in an attempt to encourage clients to help themselves. People – working is a set of techniques that focuses on clients' relationships with the wider socio – economic environment and as such it is often associated with the economic and political goals of clients. In addition, there is a concentration on methodological issues – how clients may solve their problems – and on sharing this methodological knowledge and relevant resources with clients. In keeping with the concepts of informed consent and communal control, people – working too is supposed to be non – directive.

At Witham Street and Feering Street NNLC's people – working role meant demonstrating to clients the wider significance of compulsory purchase orders; explaining the potential relevance of conducting surveys; and advising clients how these surveys could be carried out. A similar process occurred with the organization of a petition presented to the local council by the Feering Street Tenants' Association, and with Witham Street Tenants' Association where NNLC explained the significance of housing action areas and advised the association about the importance of encouraging other tenants within such areas to form into organized groups. At Wharf Mews the need to renegotiate the tenancy agreement was clear to all, but the choice to deal directly with the housing association was based on NNLC advice that this route offered a better chance of success than dealing with the housing trust, which was in effect the housing association's agent on the estate. At Stone – Blackwood Tenants' Cooperative NNLC's people – working focused on explaining to the members the role of a cooperative as a collective mechanism for securing decent housing.

In essence, people – working is part and parcel of informed consent; it is a method through which people may evaluate options put before them. Whereas informed consent leads to decisions about *what* course of action to pursue, people – working gives information on *how* to put the selected option into practical effect. In this sense, people – working is also closely linked to communal control for it is a means by which clients potentially exercise control over the selection of solutions for the problems they face. Moreover, given that people – working is also committed to providing information to clients about the wider socio – economic context of their grievances, it may be that clients pursue activities within or devoted to that wider context and not simply confined to the immediate problem in hand. This so – called 'spillover' effect was, in fact, quite limited and it is a matter to which I shall return when addressing the issue of client competence.

Client Competence

Interviews with samples of the memberships from the four housing groups indicated that there had been an increase in client competence. They attributed its development not only to their active involvement in the running of their respective groups, but also to their participation in the particular activities of their own groups. At Feering Street and Witham Street tenants' associations direct participation took the form of the successful completion of extensive surveys of members' housing needs and the state of disrepair of dwellings. A similar survey of housing need took place at Stone – Blackwood Tenants' Cooperative. At Feering Street tenants were also involved, following being taken into council ownership, in continuing negotiations with the council about the rehabilitation of the properties in the street. Being determined that the rehabilitation plans should satisfy the needs of its members, the association negotiated a system of joint consultation with the housing department. Witham Street Tenants' Association conducted a thorough survey of its members' needs and evolved a system of street representatives to ensure the interchange of important information throughout the membership. In addition, it successfully used the threat of public health legislation to push the council into beginning repairs on some of the worst affected houses. It also successfully took a case to the Rent Tribunal, and printed its own monthly newsletter. Finally, the Witham Street group secured representation on the housing sub – committee that was discussing future plans for the housing action area in which the street was located.

The competence of the members of the Stone – Blackwood Tenants' Cooperative essentially grew in relation to their involvement in the day – to – day running of the organization, the allocation of dwellings, the gathering of information on members' housing needs, and in negotiating with the local council about renovation plans for the properties the cooperative was to receive.

The activities of members at Wharf Mews Tenants' Association soon developed into promoting a variety of social and communal activities, such as setting up its own community centre, publishing a monthly newsletter, arranging barbecues and social functions, acquiring a sports pitch, etc. On the housing front, it helped to choose the estate's new management officer after it had convinced the housing association to dispense with the services of the housing trust. The tenants' association also gained representation on the board of the housing association where it continued to look after the interests of its members by negotiating on repair and heating issues.

Many of the activities described above required some legal knowledge or appreciation of legal procedures, especially those related to CPOs, tenancy agreements, and public health legislation. To the extent that individual members of the respective housing groups were active participants in these kinds of activities, it can be argued that their levels of legal competence and awareness were enlarged. Other activities, however, were more general – possibly political in nature – and may be related to a form of political competence. To what extent can one recognize the development of both legal and political competence among the clients of NNLC?

Nonet referred to legal competence as the ability to affirm the legitimacy of one's rights, to seek the recognition of one's claims, and to hold officials accountable. Clearly, such legal competence was exhibited by the four housing groups whose members articulated their grievances and selected particular strategies as a way of trying to gain the rights to which they felt entitled. Many of these strategies were legally competent but did any of the members exhibit any *political* competence? That is to say; was there any 'spillover' effect?

Nonet argued that there are important similarities between legal and political competence and some of the activities of the four housing groups could arguably be classified as operating within the political sphere. NNLC acted not only as a legal resource to groups, but also it provided information about the wider socio – economic context of those groups' housing problems. However, there appeared to be very little political competence being exhibited and few signs of the spillover effect in which individuals or groups developed skills and expertise outside the original setting. While all four groups continued to function as well – organized and cohesive bodies, only a small number of individuals ventured into activities beyond those directly concerned with their respective tenants' groups. At Feering Street only the chairman took part in wider activities; in his case, a radio programme. He also advised people in the locality on the running of their own tenants' association. A similar process occurred at Witham Street Tenants' Association where a handful of members helped to advise others on organizing a tenants' group. At Stone – Blackwood Tenants' Cooperative there were *plans*, but no more than this, to pursue activities outside the housing field.

None of this is to deny that the groups did not develop their respective organizational capabilities, nor that their members did not grow in legal awareness and competence, but it does suggest that the groups did not progress beyond the housing field. The progression from tenant cooperative to a cooperative housing association is no mean achievement, but it is a linear development in that it is restricted to a single housing issue – the provision of decent accommodation for the group's members. Moreover, each of the groups chose to pursue institutionalized channels of negotiation and consultation. This was entirely appropriate and reasonable, but it was a way of acting more in keeping with the formal, more focused, aspects of legal procedure and legal competence than with action on a wider, more political, scale where more controversial and less certain forms of action are initiated.

At Wharf Mews the picture is somewhat different. The association may be said to have moved quickly beyond the housing sphere into activities connected with the social and communal wishes of its members. However, I do not think that activities in these fields are properly classified as spillover effects in the political sense. After the initial renegotiation of the tenancy agreement the association was not again in significant conflict with its landlords. Unlike two groups in dispute with private landlords and subsequently the council over the issue of repairs, and unlike the tenants' cooperative that sought greater control over the properties it received, Wharf Mews Tenants' Association enjoyed a largely consensual relationship with its housing association about the future of the estate. Although the tenants were successful in setting up social and communal activities these were not political activities, and the skills and competences of the members in implementing these activities cannot be seen as examples of political competence.

The spillover effect at Wharf Mews was not related to the exercise of political competence since the group was not trying to assert its rights in the face of opposition from other agencies, nor was it attempting to hold officials accountable. The social programmes on the estate were in the main internal arrangements. Furthermore, there was little spillover effect with the other three groups. It would appear, therefore, at least on the evidence of NNLC's proactive approach, that while groups are prepared to pursue a number of strategies to solve problems, they prefer to use relatively institutionalized and accepted courses of action. They appeared to eschew, for the most part, wide–ranging political action, and in this sense there was little evidence to suggest the development of political competence among group members.

Communal Control

Johnson's definition of communal control referred to that situation in which the client or consumer defined his own needs and the manner in which they would be met. Communal control is, therefore, linked to the concepts of informed consent and people–working, and to the ability of an agency such as NNLC to operate in a non–directive way as an enabler. However, as an organizer of people the centre has operated in a directive fashion. Of course, it cannot force individuals to organize but where it has successfully encouraged them to form cohesive groups NNLC must soon after abandon its initial directive function if group members are to take on responsibilities for themselves. To what extent did NNLC realize a form of communal control in its dealings with groups?

On the whole the four tenants' groups did not challenge the advice given to them by NNLC on legal matters. Indeed, it might be said that groups probably had no way of knowing if all the options had been laid before them by the law centre staff. Even so, groups did appear to exercise control in two ways. First, there were decisions of principle that group members took in relation to the options and advice set out by the law centre. Decisions of principle were those taken by Feering Street Tenants' Association when its members opted to remain living locally rather than to seek alternative accommodation; when the Wharf Mews tenants decided to renegotiate their tenancy agreement; when the members of the Witham Street group opted for council ownership and rehabilitation of their properties; and when the Stone–Blackwood cooperative chose a democratic and accountable structure for the running of the group and the allocation of dwellings. These decisions of principle not only led to particular, selected, courses of action, but also clearly symbolized the initial willingness of group members to cooperate with NNLC in seeking solutions to their collective grievances. Without such decisions of principle being taken it is difficult to see how any group would cohere and persist for any length of time.

Second, there was the control that these groups exercised over the conduct of their affairs when NNLC was no longer actively involved. In each case there came a time at which NNLC withdrew from active involvement in the running of the group, but each group continued to function. It was the members who were responsible for decisions about future strategies. Thus, Feering Street and Witham Street tenants decided to maintain their efforts to ensure that the local council renovated their properties in an acceptable fashion. Wharf Mews tenants expanded their activities into social and communal fields, while at Stone – Blackwood cooperative the members decided to stay as a small organization able to respond sensitively to the needs of its membership.

In these respects one could recognize aspects of communal control in the decision – making processes of the tenants' groups, although one might describe the overall contact between NNLC and groups as one embodying a relationship based on the idea of a partnership rather than on the full implementation of the concept of communal control. Moreover, there was no communal control in the sense of groups having direct control over the policies and operational philosophy of the law centre itself. This was due to the absence of a properly constituted management committee composed of the consumers of NNLC's services.

Such a management committee is potentially a vehicle for the interchange of information between law centre staff and the people they serve. It is also a mechanism through which the overall policy of a law centre may be set by the consumers themselves. NNLC staff had lived within the centre's catchment area for some years and participated in a variety of ways in the affairs of the locality. They argued that they felt integrated into the area through a network of personal contacts and cooperative efforts, which also influenced the kinds of decisions they took in relation to the work of the law centre. They maintained that certain directions for the work of the centre emerged out of many discussions between themselves and local people. Certainly, NNLC staff were well – informed members of the local community, and they realized the importance of valid information if the law centre were to intervene successfully in local issues. They were, however, worried by the absence of a proper and formal management committee.

The absence of a management committee lasted until the end of 1976, when the eleven volunteer solicitors and community workers who ran the weekly advice sessions were formed into a committee to control the centre (NNLC, 1975 – 7:10). However, such a committee was not composed of actual consumers or clients, and decisions to engage with particular groups or on certain projects remained still in the hands of the full – time staff. To the extent that these decisions were partially the product of the staff's integration into and understanding of local affairs, consumers may, very loosely, be said to have influenced such decisions. However, it cannot be said that consumers exercised any effective control over NNLC's policy – making process.

Thus, while there are participatory emphases and some elements of communal control operating in the centre's relationship with local groups, the overall policy directions of the centre remained firmly in the hands of the professional staff. Given that all law centres, and the proactive ones in particular, lay great stress on properly constituted management committees, the lack of such a structure at NNLC was a serious omission.

Party Upgrading and Client Participation

The two final goals of NNLC are party upgrading and client participation both of which have important interlinked consequences for clients and for this reason I shall deal with them together.

Galanter referred to party upgrading as a means by which groups could secure the accountability of officials and ensure their participation in decision – making processes, which were relevant to the lives of the group members. Such accountability and participation need not only apply to the courts, but also to other dispute – resolving forums. Party upgrading allows clients to enjoy the benefits of organizational 'repeat – players'; namely, to act in a coordinated fashion, to share risks, to employ long – run strategies, etc., – all of which are more difficult for an individual acting alone.

Furthermore, party upgrading is linked to the participatory emphases described by Hadley and Hatch in Chapter One. The participatory approach requires cooperative efforts between agencies supplying services and those people consuming them. It is an approach that recognizes the knowledge of the non – expert as well as the practical community – based experience of clients. An agency such as NNLC wishing to adopt a participatory approach must develop flexible staff roles and encourage an active relationship with its clientele. The argument is that such an approach is potentially more innovative and capable of promoting self – reliant and competent clients. However, while NNLC may be in a position to claim some success for the implementation of party upgrading and of the participatory approach, it has also experienced significant failures in these fields.

In October 1973 NNLC became aware of the bad state of repair of many houses owned by a housing trust in Ashby Square. At a meeting arranged by NNLC the tenants expressed much dissatisfaction with the poor repair and with the housing trust itself. The tenants formed themselves into the Ashby Square Tenants' Association and decided to survey the extent of disrepair. It was only able to do so, however, with the close and continuing support of a student on a temporary placement with NNLC. As a result of the efforts of the student and NNLC staff the housing trust was persuaded to pay compensation to those tenants who had to vacate their homes while repairs were being carried out. Shortly afterwards the association renamed itself the Ashby Square Community Association in which there emerged two distinct viewpoints. A dozen tenants wanted to continue to focus on the repairs issue, while another thirty were more interested in providing communal facilities. Neither group could work with the other and serious conflicts developed. When the student on placement left the community association rapidly fell into decline and ceased to function. In effect, NNLC had failed to achieve party upgrading and a participatory relationship for there was no single shared need among the tenants of the square. The group had been incorrectly identified as a potential vehicle for limited social change, and far from enjoying affective, interpersonal relations the group's relationships were characterized by conflict and a lack of solidarity. No indigenous leadership or client competence emerged since the activities of the group members depended too much on the work of the student. NNLC managed to create briefly an organized group but it failed to implement its enabling role; it failed to encourage group members to act in a united and collective fashion and, as a result, the group soon ceased to exist.

Another failure of the proactive approach concerned the residents of Mentley Avenue who in March 1973 the centre invited to a public meeting to discuss the issues of disrepair, rent increases, and security of tenure. About forty people attended the meeting at which NNLC explained the implications of the forthcoming Fair Rents Act. The tenants also expressed their grievances about the poor state of repair of many of their homes. It was decided to form the Mentley Avenue Tenants' Association and each member agreed to provide a list of his or her complaints. At a subsequent meeting two weeks later, attended by representatives of the local council and the then public health department, arrangements were made in the light of the supplied lists for each tenant to be visited by a public health officer. When these visits had been completed several weeks later the company owning the properties in the avenue was presented with a number of essential repairs to be carried out according to the public health orders with which the company had been served. At this stage many tenants felt they had won their battle to have their homes properly repaired, and attendance at the association's meetings declined heavily. In April 1974 the property company sold its holdings to the local council. NNLC tried to revive interest in the tenants' association and another student on placement with the law centre acted as a liaison. Despite being taken into council ownership no repairs were carried out on the properties. Moreover, even though NNLC and the student tried to encourage the tenants' association to seek action on the delay, it fell into decline and disbanded.

Once again, NNLC failed to implement its enabling function and no self-reliant organized group developed. NNLC's attempt to upgrade the tenants into a cohesive entity was a similar failure. While these two examples highlight the problems of making a reality of party upgrading and of implementing a participatory relationship, NNLC has enjoyed a more successful outcome with the four tenants' groups described earlier. Here NNLC created party upgrading in the sense that each of the four groups became an *organized* group with the potential to benefit from being a repeat-player. Being an organized group not only facilitated certain activities, such as conducting surveys, but also it provided a ready point of contact for other bodies, such as the local council, housing associations, etc. The fact of being an organization helped these groups in their negotiations with other bodies and it helped too to represent them as being appropriate entities with which to enter into negotiations.

In terms of trying to implement a participatory relationship between itself and group members, NNLC has sought the active cooperation of groups; it has recognized and mobilized members' own lay-knowledge, and it has striven to promote self-reliant and competent clients. In this way NNLC has tried to forge an active relationship with its clientele and to respond sensitively to local needs. Thus, while NNLC has enjoyed some success in realizing both party upgrading and the participation of clients in the running of their own groups, and in securing some involvement for the groups in relevant decision-making forums, there is a structural limitation that applies to these achievements, particularly the last one.

For instance, Feering Street and Witham Street tenants' associations were dependent on the decision of the council to seek CPOs. If the council had not been so minded, it is difficult to see how either group could have forced the council to take such a decision. Moreover, both groups were relatively powerless to force the council to carry out the necessary repairs quickly and in accordance with the wishes of the groups' members. Wharf Mews Tenants' Association was not in conflict with the housing association after the tenancy renegotiation so one cannot tell how the housing association might have responded to tenants' demands that it did not wish to concede. At Stone-Blackwood Tenants' Cooperative the desire to become an housing association in its own right was stimulated by the lack of control members felt they exercised over their properties.

Even when these kinds of groups combine their own resources with those of NNLC they still face potentially powerful opponents, which includes the local council if it chooses to be so. Tenants' associations, especially with issues of repair, are limited in what they can achieve. They are weak in comparison with the local council, and also a local council may have insufficient resources to carry out repairs swiftly. In these circumstances a council may use delaying tactics, especially if there are a number of local groups seeking resources for essential repairs. The strategies available to groups and to law centres such as NNLC to overcome these delays are not very effective in general terms, although there are obviously some specific exceptions to this rule.

Organizational advocacy as conducted by NNLC in partnership with local groups, and the participation of those groups in decision – making forums – even if partial – are important developments in any proactive and participatory approach. However, they are not guarantees of success, for there are structural factors impinging on the proactive approach in a localized context that may limit the extent of social change small community groups can achieve. That said, there are, however, indications that NNLC's proactive style was able to encourage significant levels of client participation *within* organized groups. The level of client participation in the decisions of *other* significant groups and the extent to which group members can hold these others/officials accountable remain more problematic. Often the extent of this kind of participation depends on external structural factors over which local groups exert little or no control.

The work of NNLC has shown some limited gains for the members of several groups with which it has been in contact. With two groups no benefits emerged at all, not even the continuation of a coherent organization. It has not been possible in the case of NNLC to study how people suffering with housing problems would have fared had their problems been serviced on an individual basis. By the same token one cannot know how much more success, if any at all, the law centre would have enjoyed had it been able to deploy significantly more resources and personnel. What can be said is that, with rare exceptions, the centre has tried consistently to live up to its proactive goals. It has enjoyed some limited success in realizing these goals in partnership with a small number of groups in the housing sphere. Moreover, the groups themselves have in general grown in organizational abilities, and their members have developed their own legal awareness and competence.

Looking to the difficulties currently facing the law centre movement, does NNLC offer any lessons for present – day policy? Indeed have the lessons provided by the experiences of UCLC and other reactive agencies been digested by current law centres? It is to these questions that I now turn.

Notes

1. In 1977 the Law Centres' Federation published *Evidence to the Royal Commission on Legal Services*, which represented a mixture of reactivity and proactivity towards which many law centres were trying to work. The general desire, therefore, in many law centres to adopt a more proactive approach – despite the difficulties of operationalizing it – is reflected in large measure within the pages of *Towards Equal Justice* and *Evidence to the Royal Commission*. Indeed, when Lambeth Law Centre – recognizing the difficulties being caused by its

open – door approach – wished to adopt a more proactive way of working, it explicitly acknowledged that the new type of work stemmed directly from *Towards Equal Justice* (Lambeth Community Law Centre, 1975 – 6:3). Although Lambeth Law Centre was not at that time particularly successful in introducing a significantly more proactive approach, it clearly had available a set of guidelines in the form of *Towards Equal Justice*, which helped to explain and justify the need to introduce a more proactive style of operation.

2.   One other proactively designed law centre existed in the UK, namely the South Wales Anti – Poverty Action Campaign (SWAPAC). SWAPAC was initiated by a consortium of community groups in S. Wales which received the bulk of its funds for the centre from the European Economic Community. The centre's proposed operation was to be one of 'outreach' tactics, working with local groups in an attempt to alleviate various aspects of poverty. It began operations in 1976 but ceased to exist some years later when it lost its EEC funding. SWAPAC was always intended to cover a wide geographical area and therefore its services were never conceived as being appropriately delivered on an individual basis. Moreover, given its goal of trying to combat poverty, a group focus was again considered the most appropriate.

3.   Some idea of the mix of resources devoted to individual casework and to proactive activities can be seen in the following information. In 1974 Newham Rights Centre handled 663 cases of all types. Of these 462 were individual cases, but 352 of them (76.2%) were referred to other agencies. Only 110 were retained at the centre for more detailed attention. Furthermore, 93 (14%) of the 663 cases were community cases: that is to say, cases that included helping to organize groups, conducting community – based research, and undertaking community education projects (Newham Rights Centre, 1974 – 5:90 and 92 – 99). In addition to the individual cases and community cases there were 78 group cases, 58 of which were retained by the centre for detailed attention. Moreover, there were a further 30 potential test cases, 27 of which were retained by the centre. It is clear, therefore, that from the outset a significant proportion of the centre's resources were directed towards proactive activities. Indeed, the centre itself has argued that the majority of its resources were devoted to non – individual cases (Newham Rights Centre, 1974 – 5:90).

In the period 1 April 1975 to 31 March 1976 the number of retained cases, out of a grand total of 584 cases of all types, was 191 (32.9%). Of the 191, 92 (15.9% of the grand total) were retained individual cases, and 99 (17%) were group, test and community cases (Newham Rights Centre, 1977:20).

109

In the following year (1 April 1976 to 31 March 1977) the total number of cases of all types increased from 584 to 846, which was partially a reflection of the centre's increased capacity to refer cases, and also of the increased need to undertake more individual casework in the field of financial and income rights. Even so, the number of *retained* individual cases was 126 (15.6%) – a percentage similar to the previous year. The number of retained group, test and communityü cases was 181 (17.7%), which was a slight increase on the previous year's total (Newham Rights Centre, 1977:21).

4.   While Brent Law Centre itself places heavy emphasis on the initiatives of local groups as a way of explaining its proactive origins and operational philosophy, other commentators have taken a somewhat different approach. Chakraborty et al (1988:35) have argued that Brent Law Centre became a resource or proactive agency supplying its services to local groups because the centre's 'catchment area was far larger than that of North Kensington, and because the available funding provided for only a small staff'.

5.   The extent to which Brent Law Centre was able to recognize the growth of individual casework as a 'problem', and then to reduce it in order to reaffirm the centre's proactive origins can be seen from the following information that refers to the numbers of individual cases taken on by the agency.

				Note
4 months Sept – December	1971	67	cases	
4 months Jan – April	1972	55		
4 months May – August	1972	67		1
4 months Sept – December	1972	89		2
4 months Jan – April	1973	127		3
4 months May – August	1973	211		4 A
4 months Sept – December	1973	188		
4 months Jan – April	1974	198		B
4 months May – August	1974	194		5
4 months Sept – December	1974	120		6 C

Notes:
1.   This first group covers the period when the Centre was working on a voluntary basis.
2.   The second group covers the period when we knew we were going to get Urban Aid but did not yet have it.
3.   The third group covers the period when we had Urban Aid but were still mainly occupied with trying to establish an office, etc.
4.   The fourth group covers the period when the office was first established...We had 3½ staff during this time...The establishment of a working office is marked with an "A"...

5.   During this period   3 further staff were employed although one left and was not replaced and the part timer was taken on for longer hours. Although further staff were taken on it was decided not to increase our intake of casework. This was (1) because we had too much already, (2) because we wanted to undertake more systematic campaigns and (3) because we wanted to increase the amount of work we were doing for local groups since this area had suffered a great deal from our casework activities. This period is marked with a "B"...

6.   This last period (marked with a "C"...) shows the decision to limit even further our casework intake...

7.   Two general comments should be made: (1) the work of the Centre has never been limited to casework and (2) our work in advising and assisting other agencies and organisations about their casework has increased as the direct casework has in effect declined (Brent Community Law Centre, 1975:44 – 5).

Unlike reactive law centres, which often found it very difficult to reduce individual caseloads and to channel freed resources into more proactive activities, Brent Law Centre was largely successful in its own attempt. This may have owed a good deal to the fact that – unlike the majority of open – door reactive centres – Brent already possessed staff who were skilled in and knowledgeable of groupwork, community education, etc. For such staff the build up of casework was not simply a matter to be deplored but an issue to be tackled in a consistent manner. The reduction in the level of individual casework freed resources that the staff were already accustomed to applying towards proactive goals. At many reactive centres, even when resources were thus freed, a more proactive approach was not always introduced because their respective staffs lacked many of the practical skills and areas of knowledge to operationalize a proactive style.

6.   SWAPAC's application for funds to the EEC was successfully based on the argument that a proactive approach was best suited to combating poverty in a relatively wide geographical area such as S. Wales.

7.   As a result of its concentration on housing issues NNLC has done only limited work in other areas; for example, a cyclists' action campaign designed to provide a safer environment for cyclists, and working with underprivileged families.

8.   The accounts of the four tenants' groups are based on several sources; a review of NNLC documents, interviews and discussions with NNLC staff, a review of documents produced by the tenants' groups themselves, and interviews with a sample from each of the groups' memberships.

6 Law centres in the present: old problems and new developments

In previous chapters I outlined the origins and development of the law centre movement throughout the 1970s, and I provided in-depth accounts of the work of UCLC and NNLC. In this chapter and the next I shall be examining the more recent state of law centres and I shall be describing many of the current difficulties facing the law centre movement. In addition I will be analysing whether the earlier work of reactive and proactive agencies, such as UCLC and NNLC, has any relevance not only for the current difficulties many centres face, but also for the future structure and role of the movement.

The Search For Secure Funding

Whereas the 1970s were a time of innovative developments within the law centre field – combined too with some unsatisfactory and often frustrating operational difficulties – the 1980s threw into stark relief the funding problems of the movement as a whole. In part, the history of the law centre movement in the 1980s is the story of its unsuccessful struggle to secure adequate and independent funding. The end of the 1980s and the beginning of a new decade appear as yet to offer no respite to the movement on the funding issue. Much of this failure to attract adequate funding must be laid at the door of central government.

Opening and Closing

In 1980 three centres in Wandsworth were closed for lack of funds. In the same year, and as a testimony to the need for law centres and to the resilience of the movement, the Law Centres' Federation (LCF) reported that another law centre had opened and a further six were on the threshold of opening (LCF, Summer 1980:5). In 1981 the law centre covering the whole of S. Wales lost its funding and ceased operations. In addition the futures of the law centres in Handsworth and Small Heath were thrown into doubt because of proposed reductions in their grants by the local authority. In the light of these mounting financial problems the Lord Chancellor's Advisory Committee on Legal Aid called for proper funding for all law centres, and argued that the centres were an essential part of the provision of legal services (Lord Chancellor's Office, 1980 – 1:101, para 68).

Despite the generally gloomy financial outlook several law centres were set up in 1981, some of them with the assistance of funds from the Greater London Council (GLC)[1]. What was to become a growing financial reliance on the GLC and other metropolitan county councils was the direct result of the reluctance of central government to save law centres from threatened closure in the short – term, and its failure to introduce a system of adequate funding in the long – term. Moreover, the abolition of the GLC and metropolitan county councils in 1986 further underlined the precarious financial position of many law centres. However, the continuing ability of new centres to open with a variety of funds cobbled together – usually on a short – term basis – demonstrated both the urgent unmet legal needs in many parts of the country and the recognition of the suitability of law centres to meet those needs.

Problems of Recruitment

In 1982 there were concerns that it was becoming increasingly difficult to recruit experienced solicitors to work in law centres. The reasons were identified as follows: 'lack of career structure, uncompetitive salaries, lack of administrative back – up, the imposition of rigid policy by the funding body and the threat of withdrawal of funds...' (LCF, Winter 1982 – 3:3). The phrase 'lack of administrative back – up' refers to the policy of self – servicing by solicitors, which has been adopted in some, but not all, law centres. The idea behind self – servicing is to prevent the domination of law centres by legal professionals by ensuring that they service a large part of their own work, such as typing their briefs, etc. The LCF has intimated that self – servicing may appear as unattractive to potential applicants who have the necessary experience (LCF, Spring 1982:1).

One law centre worker has posed the question somewhat differently. The movement may have problems attracting experienced solicitors, but it has no difficulties attracting those who are relatively

113

inexperienced. The real question is why is the movement unable to retain these professionals. This law centre worker argues the answer to this question is to be found in the training solicitors receive, which leaves them ill – equipped to handle the realities of law centre work (Law Centres' Federation, Autumn 1982:4).

For its part, the Lord Chancellor's Advisory Committee commented that while it was a tribute to the morale of law centre staff who had to operate on restricted funds, nevertheless, 'there have been increasing problems of recruiting and retaining qualified staff; there has been an inability to carry out long – term planning and far too much effort has had to be put into assuring year – to – year survival' (Lord Chancellor's Office, 1983 – 4:338 – 9, para 416).

Central Government Funding and the Views of the LCF

In 1982 the Department of the Environment was providing approximately three – quarters of the funds for roughly three – quarters of all law centres via various parts of the Urban Aid scheme (LCF, Spring 1982:6). In December 1982 the department decided to defer applications for funding for new law centres under the Urban Programme, and to renew existing centres' grants only for one year at a time. This decision, coupled with the government's low priority for funding social projects, increased the financial vulnerability of law centres, and there were fears of severe cutbacks or even closures at several London centres and at Newcastle, Leeds, and Birmingham (LCF, Winter 1982 – 3:8).

There were three responses in 1983 to this deterioration in the financial position of law centres. The Lord Chancellor's Advisory Committee argued that:

> Law centres are properly regarded as part of nationwide legal services. Some contribution from local authorities might continue to be appropriate – perhaps on the 75% – 25% basis of the Urban Programme. But the 'pump – priming' basis of the Urban Programme should give way to more assured support, entailing for central government a more permanent, though modest, commitment of resources (Lord Chancellor's Office, 1982 – 3:174, para 172).

The second reaction came from the government in November 1983 in the form of its long – awaited response to the report of the Royal Commission on Legal Services, which gave the government an opportunity to tackle the issue of funding for law centres. The entirely woeful and inadequate response was that the recommendations of the RCLS were 'under consideration; an announcement will be made in due course' (Lord Chancellor's Office, November 1983:8). The next report of the Lord Chancellor's Advisory Committee commented that as far as the funding of law centres was concerned, the government 'lacked any commitment to a unified approach' (Lord Chancellor's Office, 1983 – 4:334, para 401).

In the light of the lack of central government commitment and the 'great insecurity and low morale amongst existing Law Centre employees', the Law Centres' Federation published in November 1983 *The Case for Law Centres*, which was a public defence of and justification for the law centre movement (LCF, November 1983:4). This third response to the financial plight of law centres was published when 25% of the LCF's total then of forty six members did not know whether they would still be funded in a year's time. *The Case for Law Centres* noted that nine out of ten UK citizens lived outside any law centre catchment area; that many deprived areas of Britain had no law centre; and that 67% of law centres depended on funds from central government departments, which nevertheless had no common and long-term policy in respect of law centre finances. It also argued that law centres were an essential element in a three-pronged approach to the delivery of legal advice and assistance, consisting of general advice agencies, such as CABx, private solicitors using the Legal Aid scheme, and law centres themselves (LCF, November 1983:1). Valuable though the first edition of *The Case for Law Centres* may have been in publicizing the position of law centres – further editions were produced in October 1985 and April 1989 – the movement was already facing new difficulties even as the document was published. In October 1983 the government announced its intention to abolish the GLC and other metropolitan county councils upon which many centres depended financially. In addition, there were concerns about further changes in the policy of the Urban Programme and about the effects of rate-capping on law centres.

Further Financial Problems and Reviews of Law Centre Operations

Streamlining the Cities, the government's white paper for the reorganization of the GLC and the metropolitan county councils (MCCs) was published in October 1983 and proposed to abolish the GLC and the six MCCs on the 1 April 1986. Little of the white paper was about law centres, which were subsumed under the category of voluntary bodies. The government proposal was that with the abolition of these upper tier authorities voluntary bodies formerly funded by them would approach borough and district councils for financial assistance (Department of the Environment, October 1983:11).

In 1984 the Law Centres' Federation published *Response to the White Paper 'Streamlining the Cities'* in which the Federation expressed its fears about the likely financial impact of the government's proposals on law centres. Chiefly, these fears were that the abolition of upper tier authorities might make law centres even more vulnerable financially, since the district authorities might be reluctant to take over in full the funding responsibilities of the GLC and MCCs for law centres. Although local authorities had legislative powers under which they could fund voluntary bodies, which according to the LCF were subject to potentially restrictive financial

115

limitations, the overall pressure on these authorities was to reduce public expenditure, especially in the light of proposed rate – capping procedures. The LCF was afraid that since local authorities 'will wish to preserve functions for which they have a statutory duty, there will be even more pressure to reduce functions which are not mandatory, such as support to voluntary organisations' (LCF, 1984:2). In what, in the event, turned out to be an overly pessimistic prediction, the LCF argued in 1984 that unless proper provision were made to replace the funding supplied by the GLC and MCCs the law centre movement could, by 1987, be reduced from forty six law centres serving six million people to thirty serving four million (LCF, 1984:2). The Law Society and the Lord Chancellor's Advisory Committee were equally concerned about the financial fate of law centres, and they both recommended alternative funding arrangements should be made (Lord Chancellor's Office, 1983 – 4:59 and 335).

In February 1984 the LCF published a *Design Brief for a National Funding Policy for Law Centres* as a further attempt to influence government policy. In June 1984 representatives of the LCF met with the Lord Chancellor's Advisory Committee to discuss the uncertain and difficult financial position of law centres. Neither of these two events was successful, and the Conservative Government's reluctance to commit funds to law centres continued unabated. Thus, the Urban Programme continued to favour capital expenditure projects to the detriment of law centres, which were social projects. In addition, the Department of the Environment switched from granting funds to law centres on a five year basis to a policy of year by year renewal, and thereby strengthened perceptions of uncertainty about future secure funding. However, once again in the middle of a depressing financial outlook, three new law centres opened up in August 1984, which increased the membership of the LCF to fifty four. In January 1985, in another encouraging development, the LCF having already moved to new London premises opened a second office in Birmingham where the full – time worker's salary was paid, ironically enough, by the Department of the Environment.

Two reviews of the work and role of law centres were completed in 1984 by the Lord Chancellor's Advisory Committee and by R.B.L.Prior of the Society of Conservative Lawyers. Both attempted to explain why law centres had not been successful in obtaining secure and adequate funding. According to Prior while one of the movement's strengths was the left – wing political persuasion of many law centre employees, this became a disadvantage when applying for central government funds (Prior, 1984:4). Prior also argued that management committees did not effectively control the activities of law centres; that some centres conducted too much group and campaign work; and that law centres had become too involved in political controversies, which had damaged their reputation (Prior, 1984:7 – 19). Generally, however, much of the pamphlet praised the overall work and achievements of the law centre movement.

Furthermore, Prior took the view that one single department of central government should bear the responsibility for ensuring secure funding for law centres (Prior, 1984:6).

The Lord Chancellor's Advisory Committee's review was more detailed than Prior's, but conveyed similar messages. The committee objected to the fact that some law centres had used legal services not on an individual basis, but as an attempt to secure social justice. In so doing these centres had operated not as complementary to the Legal Aid scheme and the private profession, but as alternatives. Pursuing such objectives had led to widespread suspicion in some quarters about the worth of law centres (Lord Chancellor's Office, 1983 – 4:341, para 424).

Having voiced its distaste for these objectives, the committee went on to argue that although this suspicion still lingered, the only proper way to evaluate law centres was to ask whether they met legal needs, which other agencies did not satisfy, and whether they did so more effectively and economically than any of the alternatives. In answering these questions the Advisory Committee clearly felt that law centres were satisfying unmet legal needs; indeed, the committee argued that more centres were necessary, especially in rural areas and in times of recession (Lord Chancellor's Office, 1983 – 4:342, para 428). In addition, the committee recommended that there was a need to ensure that law centres 'be more fully integrated into the legal services network, and should no longer have to depend upon meagre, uncertain, and uncoordinated funding (Lord Chancellor's Office, 1983 – 4:343, para 429).

The year ended with repeated demands for secure and adequate funding for law centres; and law centres might, therefore, have expected that 1985 would see some progress towards the realization of this goal. They were to be disappointed.

Parliamentary Debates on the Future of Law Centres

Fresh prospects, of cut – backs or closure hung over many law centres in 1985[2]. Opening a debate in the House of Lords, Lord Elwyn – Jones – the Lord Chancellor in the last Labour Government – referred to the 'steady retreat' by the Urban Programme from the funding of law centres, and he urged the government to act so as to prevent any possible closures of law centres (Parliamentary Debates, House of Lords, May 1985: col 720). Lords Pitt and Gifford outlined the achievements of law centres and called on the government to provide proper funding. Lord Skelmersdale replied on behalf of the Conservative Government explaining that:

decisions on the need for law centres are essentially local matters. The local authorities are the public sector bodies best placed to judge whether or not to give support. We have no proposals to set up a specific source of central funding for law centres (Parliamentary Debates, House of Lords, May 1985: col 728).

The debate ended before there could be any discussion of how reasonable it was to expect local authorities to fund law centres in the light of the forthcoming abolition of the GLC and MCCs, and in the light of the effects of rate – capping on local authority expenditure.

If the government felt that it had not made its point sufficiently clear in the Lords, the Attorney – General explained to a Commons committee that law centres 'should be funded locally according to the local perception of the need for them, and within the constraints of local resources' (Parliamentary Debates, House of Commons, Standing Committee D, July 1985: col 233). The Lord Chancellor's Advisory Committee felt forced, once again, to complain about this apparent governmental indifference towards law centres (Lord Chancellor's Office, 1984 – 5:85, para 99)[3].

A small protest group composed of law centre staff, clients, and management committee members ushered in 1986 with a lunchtime vigil outside the offices of the Lord Chancellor's Department in an attempt to break the government's intransigence over the funding issue[4]. Although photographs of some of them in *Law Centres' News* made them look jovial enough, their spirits must surely have been dampened by the tenor of two parliamentary debates held some weeks later. Lord Elwyn – Jones once again set before the House of Lords in February 1986 the reasons for central government support of law centres. He outlined the financial problems and uncertainties facing many of them with the impending abolition of upper tier authorities, and he argued that the government's transitional arrangements for the funding of voluntary projects by lower tier councils after the abolition of the GLC and MCCs were inadequate (Parliamentary Debates, House of Lords, 17 February 1986: cols 476 – 8). Replying again for the government, Lord Skelmersdale stated that the majority of successful time – expired Urban Programme projects did, in fact, receive replacement funds from local authorities. Moreover, he argued that the government had already shown its support for law centres, which amounted in 1985 – 6 to £2.2 million in Urban Programme grants to twenty eight law centres, with a further £628,000 from the Lord Chancellor's Department in direct funding for seven law centres. This department could not, however, take over responsibility for the funding of all law centres since it lacked the administrative and financial resources to do so (Parliamentary Debates, House of Lords, 17 February 1986: cols 493 – 4). Thus, law centres, stated Lord Skelmersdale,

> must seek support on a local basis from local authorities by convincing those authorities that, at a time of public expenditure constraint...their services are sufficiently valuable to merit local authority funding (Parliamentary Debates, House of Lords, 17 February 1986: col 492).

A Commons debate in the following March served only to allow some members of the lower house to reiterate the arguments in favour of law centres, and to receive the same response from the Solicitor – General who maintained that central government would not assume any direct or general responsibility for law centres (Parliamentary Debates, House of Commons, 13 March 1986: col 1252).

Throughout the period 1980–6 law centres experienced a 'piecemeal' kind of financial existence, with many centres not knowing whether next month or next year they would continue to be funded adequately, or whether they would be closed, or whether they would face severe cutbacks. At one stage it appeared as if the abolition of the GLC and MCCs in April 1986 would mean decimation for law centres. Only through the constant efforts of individual law centres and their supporters and through the tireless lobbying of the LCF, aided by the funds that many local authorities have put up either willingly or after some persuasion, has the movement avoided that fate. However, one should not assume that the financial position after April 1986 was an adequate and secure one.

Continuing Financial Difficulties And Their Effects On The Work Of Law Centres

Currently there is continuing and widespread anxiety in many law centres concerning the adequacy and security of their funding arrangements. It is by no means uncommon for centres to exist on a year–to–year basis, for many local authorities are unwilling to commit funds in the long–term when there are so many competing demands for funding from the voluntary sector. While this makes financial sense to the funding bodies, it does nothing to reduce the levels of uncertainty within the law centre movement, nor does it allow many centres to engage in longer–term planning. The movement as a whole cannot make the progress it would otherwise expect in meeting the needs of its clientele when a major area of its activities is the constant struggle to obtain funding.

Insufficient and insecure funding has had, and continues to have, deleterious effects on the quantity and quality of services to clients; on the efforts to recruit and retain staff; and on the pace at which law centres can respond to new developments in the field of poverty law. For some centres, a shortage of funds has meant an increasing reliance on pursuing those cases that can generate income from the Legal Aid system. This development runs the risk of increasing bureaucratization within law centres as a result of the greater administrative procedures that have to be carried out. Moreover, it also implies a greater frequency of means–testing; something that law centres in the past have sought to avoid as much as possible. The Lord Chancellor's Advisory Committee commented:

> In practice, in recent years, many law centres have been compelled to maximize their Legal Aid and Green Form income simply to ensure survival. This is an unwelcome development. It detracts from the key role of law centres as providers of services which the private profession

cannot offer. Until, however, centres receive assured block grant funding, Legal Aid income will necessarily continue to constitute a significant part of their finances (Lord Chancellor's Office, 1983 – 4:345, para 436).

Ironically, in 1989, doubts about the future operation of the Legal Aid Board and how law centres might be affected under the new bidding system had been expressed by several law centres. The possibility was raised that law centres might no longer be able to generate sufficient Legal Aid income as many of them had done prior to the creation of the Legal Aid Board.

It would be extremely useful to highlight the consequences of the general shortage of funds by drawing on examples from a range of law centres' annual reports.

Quality and Quantity of Services

'It has been one of the most difficult years in the law centre's history' is a typical and recurring theme in the annual reports of many law centres in the late 1980s[5]. Numerous centres reported that their staffs were working under increasing pressure and that there appeared to be no prospect of an imminent improvement in this situation. On the contrary, as Greenwich Community Law Centre (1988:1) commented, its funding position continued to be difficult because the centre was 'affected by the constraints on local government spending. The position will become more serious in the next financial year'.

Hyson Green Law Centre (1987 – 8:3 and 11 – 13) highlighted how it continued to provide a service to clients despite the lack of adequate funding and the increasing burden of new legislation to which the centre was responding. Much of the centre's efforts, however, depended on the work of unpaid individuals, students on placements, and workers on the Community Programme. Without in any way criticizing the value of these individuals' work, it would seem that desperate financial circumstances may have made the centre rather over – dependent on such people. Plumstead Community Law Centre (1987 – 8:1) also reported unremitting pressure on its staff, which was only managed through the commitment of both the staff and volunteer advisers.

At Avon and Bristol Community Law Centre (1988:2) a more desperate battle was waged, and ultimately won, against impending closure as a result of the withdrawal of Urban Aid funding from April 1988. Even though the centre received replacement funding from the local authority, at a time when the authority itself was facing financial difficulties, the work of the centre has been hampered by being severely understaffed and by the increase in demand for its services. A similar cut in central government funds at the North Manchester Law Centre (1987:3), which subsequently was funded by its local council, led to the centre giving up its advice sessions at two locations within its catchment area. In contrast, at the South Manchester Law Centre (1988:3) the fears the staff had for the financial year ending April 1988 did not become reality, but only as a result of the staff ensuring that all Legal Aid bills were submitted to provide extra income.

Wolverhampton Law Centre (1987 – 8:4 – 6) experienced an increased demand for its services at a time when its future funding by the local council was in doubt. As a consequence of this uncertainty, the centre reported a decline in its services, a reduction in opening hours, and a severe restriction on accepting new cases. This theme of increased demand coupled with a reduction in financial and other resources has become a common one in the tales of woe that emerge from the country's law centres[6]. For instance, Stockwell and Clapham Law Centre (1988:1) admitted that it was unable to respond to the increased demands it faced.

> Both of our main funders, Lambeth Council and the Inner London Education Authority, have dealt with their own financial difficulties by making cuts in their financial support to the Law Centre. We have lost £14,000 in the current year. This has meant that some staff who have left have not been replaced. The remaining staff are, as a result, stretched to the limit.

In similar manner, Saltley Action Centre (1987 – 8:2) stated that 'the Centre's actual funding fell well short of needs. The paradox remains whilst work – loads increase, funding in real terms does not.'

Such can be the shortage of funds that the quality of service provided by law centres is often finely balanced and easily disturbed[7]. Thus, at Roehampton and Putney Community Law Centre (1987 – 8:4) when two workers took maternity leave there were no additional funds to employ locum staff and, as a result, the centre had to reduce its welfare rights cases. Other centres have fared even worse with North Kensington Law Centre (1987:2) reporting that in 1986 – 7 a deficit of nearly £17,000 severely depleted its cash reserves, which in turn meant that staff posts were frozen, wage levels could not be increased to acceptable levels, and the centre's out – of – hours emergency service was shut down. Sadly, even this poor state of affairs can be 'improved on'. When the London Borough of Islington was forced to reduce its expenditure by £30m the South Islington Law Centre was in the direct line of fire. The council resolved to cut the budget of the centre by 20% from April 1989, and to cut North Islington Law Centre's budget by 10%. 'By any measurement, a 20% reduction in revenue income represents a crisis' (South Islington Law Centre, 1987 – 8:5).

Some law centres face not sudden and severe cuts in funding, but rather what Brighton Law Centre (1988:3) refers to as an 'annual struggle for survival'. Others, such as Liverpool 8 Law Centre (1987 – 8:7), rely to some extent on charitable funds – the Liverpool centre receives no money at all from its local council and depends entirely on charitable income – but unfortunately the sources of charitable funds 'are continually drying up'. However, the financial picture although generally a depressing one is not without some encouraging developments.

For instance, Paddington Law Centre actually closed in March 1986 due to lack of funds, but it was reopened in October with a grant from the London Boroughs Grants Committee (Paddington Law Centre, 1986 – 7:3). The fortunes of the Hillingdon Legal Resource Centre (1986 – 7:1) were also revived with the receipt of funds from this same body and from its local council in 1986. Dudley Law Centre (1987 – 8:1) lost its Urban Aid grant in 1988 but received continued financial support from its own borough council. Similar strong support came from Warrington Community Law Centre's local council. Although the law centre had been unsuccessful in its application for monies to the European Social Fund, the council provided additional finance in order that the centre could maintain existing staffing levels (Warrington Community Law Centre, 1987 – 8:Foreword). In a similar happy vein, after negotiations with several councils in the area the Stockton on Tees Law Centre (1988:1) was able to fund the creation of a new centre in Hartlepool. While in Gloucester a public campaign in 1988 succeeded in committing the local council to the full funding of the Gloucester Law Centre (1987 – 8:10). Finally, in Middlesbrough the borough council told its local law centre that it was unlikely to cease its funding in the near future.

> This assurance has released the time of staff at the Law Centre, who were previously 'chasing money' for parts of the year, enabling them to undertake other essential work linked to the provision of the Law Centre's Services as opposed to the Financing of those services (Middlesbrough Law Centre, 1988: unnumbered).

I shall return to the question of finance presently, but the general shortage of funds – alleviated by a few 'success' stories where councils have been somewhat more generous – has not only affected the quality and quantity of services; it has also influenced recruitment.

Recruitment and Retention of Law Centre Staff

Given the picture, which has emerged from the previous section, of many law centres struggling to make financial ends meet, it would not be surprising if they also suffered problems to do with the recruitment and retention of suitably qualified staff. The following are examples of such problems, which are becoming increasingly typical throughout the law centre movement.

> The local authority actually cut our grant this year by over five thousand pounds instead of increasing it to meet rising costs. We are a firm of Solicitors in effect and have in terms of recruitment to compete with the private sector in securing staff. We have to pay well below minimum levels for all our workers. The Centre needs to pay better salaries to keep qualified and experienced staff and in the future it needs to recruit the same to maintain

both the quantity and real quality of its present work (Tower Hamlets Law Centre, 1987 – 8:2). Tower Hamlets has not only had to cope with inadequate premises, but also it has had to rely for its very survival in 1987 – 8 on donations from private companies. Its annual report for 1987 – 8 even carried a covenant form to allow individuals to make their own donations. The centre's treasurer argued that he couldn't see the centre having the capacity to survive in the following year without the need to make major cuts in services (Tower Hamlets Law Centre, 1987 – 8:28).

Such funding uncertainties have prompted several law centres to remark – for instance, Wolverhampton Law Centre (1987 – 8:10) – that 'professionally qualified people are unlikely to be attracted to an organisation which does not have an assured future'. Moreover, as Southall Community Law Centre (1987 – 8:1) has pointed out, the financial position of law centres 'is a source of great anxiety to all people working in voluntary organisations – a fact borne out by the difficulty encountered in recruiting and retaining well – qualified staff'. The centre lacked a three – year qualified solicitor for part of the year, which severely inhibited its ability to earn Legal Aid monies. Finally, these uncertainties not only lead to problems in recruitment and retention of staff, but also they hinder the ability of law centres to engage in effective planning to meet the changing and growing needs of their clientele (Brighton Law Centre, 1988:3).

Law centres are heavily dependent on local authorities to supply their funds. They attempt to make up the shortfalls in funding from local councils in a number of ways; company and individual donations, charities, fund – raising events, and – as the experience of Southall Law Centre has already suggested – Legal Aid income.

Legal Aid and Law Centres

I have already argued that the increased frequency of legally – aided cases at law centres has added to the levels of means – testing and bureaucratic procedures, neither of which are in the interests of the centres[8]. For example, North Kensington Law Centre (1987:2) admitted that it had increasingly turned to Legal Aid income as a way of balancing its books. 'This not only means our work priorities being distorted towards work on which we can earn legal aid at the expense of work we cannot, but imposes an extra administrative burden on our staff'. However, during times of severe financial hardship law centres must raise income where they can[9]. Even here, however, new doubts have arisen about the long – term value of Legal Aid to law centres. Hammersmith and Fulham Law Centre (September 1989:3) argue that:

> The Legal Aid Board, which now administers Legal Aid, seems to expect Law Centres to undertake specialist areas of casework, and be paid on the same individual client basis as a legal aid firm of solicitors. This would be a giant step backwards, because at the moment Law

Centres, which receive grants from local and central government, are not completely shackled to the private enterprise logic of profit. If a client needs extra time, or a particular legal problem deserves attention, then at present Law Centres can provide a limited service in those areas – irrespective of whether legal aid or private wealth is prepared to pay.

The Board might also pay Centres to provide other sorts of legal services – to community groups, on specific projects, etc, but this would certainly be on a more restricted and less flexible basis than at present. The independence of Law Centres, and their ability to respond to the local need for advice and representation would be greatly undermined. It would no longer be the locally – elected Management Committee deciding what work the Centre carried out, but a distant quango.

Similar fears were raised by several law centres and by the Law Society about the future operation of the new Legal Aid system. The Legal Aid Act 1988 created the Legal Aid Board with a remit to make proposals for changing the operation of the Green Form scheme, (the Legal Advice and Assistance scheme). At the time of writing, the Board was engaged in consultation with various bodies in the legal services field before finalizing its proposals. However, some of the proposals are already known such as the recommendation that the Board would entertain 'bids' from private solicitors' firms and advice and law centres to provide legal advice. The Board would, in effect, grant franchises for Green Form work, and there is a possibility that law centres might be permitted to apply for welfare law franchises (Law Society, August 1989:6). The Board has taken over the responsibility from the Lord Chancellor's Department for the funding of seven law centres directly, but not as a part of any future franchising system. The future position of these centres is not yet decided.

The question of whether law centres should apply for a franchise raises the question of the role of the Legal Aid Board in the management of centres they fund either through franchises or directly... (Law Society, August 1989:25).

The Law Society is clear in its own mind that the Solicitors' Practice Rules would forbid any majority representation of the Board in the management of law centres. It would be permitted one representative on a law centre's management committee, but no more.

Even so, many law centres are anxious about the future role of the Legal Aid Board. Greenwich Community Law Centre (1988:6) stated that if advice agencies bid for a grant to carry out all advice work in a particular area on specific topics, such as welfare rights, this may lead to the withdrawal of the Green Form scheme from those agencies that were unsuccessful in their bids to the Board.

This would undermine a law centre's work in important service areas if it were denied the right to use the scheme. Moreover: The government says that Law Centres should be funded locally. If other advice agencies or local firms tender for the advice work the local authority may cut funding to Law Centres. If Law Centres decide to compete for tendering they will have to ditch their project work and most of their existing type of casework to make a living from the advice work contract, and become more like an advice centre...There are many issues here and they are still being hotly debated. Whatever happens we need to be active in evaluating what the various scenarios might mean...(Greenwich Community Law Centre, 1988:17).

Although the Board's decisions on the future of the Green Form scheme and other matters are not yet finalized, the uncertainty concerning their implications for law centres has already affected the funding policies and attitudes of some local authorities and charities (Central London Community Law Centre Ltd, 1987–8:4). For law centres themselves, the great fear is that many of them will not be in a sufficiently strong position to tender for the contracts to provide legal advice in given geographical areas. As a result they may be denied income from the Green Form scheme on which a great many law centres have become increasingly reliant as a means of supplementing inadequate grants (Saltley Action Centre, 1987–8:3).

In the midst of pressing financial circumstances many law centres have had to make various cuts in their services, but they have not stagnated. New developments have taken place within law centres even as many of them struggle each year to survive.

Responding To Need: New Developments In Law Centres

The development of new specialisms and services in law centres is naturally constrained by the availability of personnel and financial resources. Within these constraints, however, law centres have remained alert to changing needs in their respective catchment areas and to the necessity to respond to them. There has been a variety of changing needs, and the movement's response has included the development of services for the mentally ill and for those who are HIV positive or who have AIDS; the creation of new advice and 'outreach' sessions; the preparation of responses to new legislation in the areas of social security, immigration, and education; the development of 'second tier' agencies; and new forms of community control.

Health Issues

In 1982 an advice and legal representation project was set up at Springfield Hospital in London, the first project to be located in a psychiatric hospital, to provide an independent and confidential service to in – patients and day – patients. It also provides training for patients and hospital staff on mental health law, welfare rights, and some other subjects (Springfield Hospital, 1986 – 8:1). Highfields and Belgrave Law Centre has also done work in this field, focusing on mental health services in Leicestershire and how these relate to the black community of the area (Highfields and Belgrave Law Centre, 1984 – 5:11). North Lewisham Law Centre (1984:1) reported a new area of its work representing people at mental health tribunals; while Wolverhampton Law Centre (1985 – 6:3) also noted an increase in its work related to mental health.

In keeping with the relatively recent emergence of AIDS among the British population, Gateshead Law Centre (1988 – 9: unnumbered) set up in 1988 a confidential advice and casework service for those whose rights have been affected because they were HIV positive or had AIDS. The centre has also been involved in group, educational and training work in this field.

Immigration and Gender Issues

Many law centres, and especially those with large populations of ethnic minorities, have been developing their expertise in the area of immigration and nationality. Some centres are also involved in the area of sex discrimination. Whereas housing problems is still the largest area of client demand in the majority of law centres, at Bradford Law Centre (1984:3 and 6) the biggest area is immigration. The Central London Law Centre (1984:20) has responded to the immigration problems of its Chinese community, while Hammersmith and Fulham Community Law Centre (1987:1) has noted the need to devote a 'massive and consistent input into immigration and nationality problems'. At Hounslow Law Centre (1983 – 4:26) in 1984 the staff were spending a major part of their time advising on people's rights under the British Nationality Act 1981. In 1987 the centre had to set up special advice sessions for clients who were confused about or made anxious by the 31 December 1987 deadline for registration under the provisions of the 1981 Act for various Commonwealth citizens (Hounslow Law Centre, 1987 – 8:11).

This increase in client demand was replicated at Wolverhampton Law Centre (1987 – 8:6) where it was noted that in the last three months of 1987 the number of nationality cases grew 'to a torrent' with long queues forming in the centre's reception area. Likewise at Tottenham Neighbourhood Law Centre (1986 – 7:2) where immigration issues and changes in social security provision brought a large increase in the centre's workload. 'There has been an almost 100% increase in clients seeking advice at our reception this year...unless we find adequate resources, it will be impossible to satisfy the expectations from the community'. In the light of such heavy client demands several centres have planned to increase their services in immigration and related areas, such as at Sheffield Law Centre (1988:2), which decided it would focus its work on the most oppressed sections of society, especially the black community. While at Salford Law Centre (1988 – 9: unnumbered) a review of the centre's activities led to a decision to give greater emphasis to the issues of racism and sexism. A similar planning exercise at Adamsdown Community Law Centre (1985 – 7:10) meant that staff attended immigration and nationality courses with a view to expanding this area of the centre's work.

Women's rights has been a growth area too in some law centres, and several of them have started women's advice sessions. Southall Community Law Centre (1984 – 5:7) has gone further and employed one member of staff whose sole responsibility is women's rights. At Avon and Bristol Law Centre (1984 – 5:2) the staff decided that 'fighting racism and sexism are work area priorities'.

Social Security, Welfare Benefits, and Advice Sessions

The introduction of the Social Security Act in April 1988 led to heavy increases in demand from clients at many law centres.

> There have been major changes in the benefit system and the Law Centre has been required to put additional resources into advice provision and training in this area (Hyson Green Law Centre, 1987 – 8:5).

This was particularly evident in the area of enquiries concerning disability benefits and the operation of the Social Fund. A similar story unfolded at other centres[10]. At Gloucester Law Centre (1987 – 8:5) the agency was forced to drop its immigration work from June 1988 in order to cope with the increased demand for advice in the welfare benefits and housing areas.

Some centres have been more fortunate and have been able to expand their services somewhat, such as the Southwark Law Project (1988:1), which provided a new walk – in advice session at a local CAB office in order to extend the centre's services more evenly throughout the borough. Others have moved into giving advice on school – related issues (Stockwell and Clapham Law Centre, 1988:2), and on debt problems (Warrington Community Law Centre, 1987 – 8; and Castlemilk Law Centre 1988 – 9). At Wolverhampton Law Centre (1988 – 9:11) civil liberties was included as a new area of work, including complaints about police misconduct.

Second Tier Agencies

The idea of a law centre acting as a second tier agency – one that supplies advice and training to other advice agencies in the locality – is not a particularly new concept, but it is one way in which some law centres have tried to deliver their services in an efficient and effective manner. One such agency is the Leicester Rights Centre (1987 – 8:i), which provides 'information, advice, consultation and training to voluntary and statutory agencies. It also undertakes some casework and research in various fields of welfare law'.

There are lesser variations on this theme of 'advising the advisers', such as may be found at Middlesbrough Law Centre where the centre has undertaken training and educational work for staff, volunteers and community groups. However, it has been restricted in how much work it could do in this area due to lack of finance. Nevertheless, it has plans to apply for funds to establish a Law Centre Training Unit for the area (Middlesbrough Law Centre, 1988: unnumbered). Gateshead Law Centre (1988 – 9: unnumbered) put on an extra advice session in conjunction with the local polytechnic's law school so that in addition to offering advice to clients the centre is also involved in helping to train future lawyers.

Changes in legislation and a deepening of poverty and homelessness have put a great deal of pressure on law centres. Thamesdown Law Centre (1988 – 9:3) has responded by emphasizing project and issue – based work that has enabled it to provide support, training, and advice to the very organizations most affected by poverty.

While all of these responses have been initiated as a result of changes in legislation or in the socio – economic position of clients, law centres have also been developing their ideas of community control through management committees. Without denying the wishes of many clients wanting to play a role in the management of their respective law centres, these changes have been more 'internally' driven than the previous ones in the sense that the realization of systems of consumer control has long been a goal of the law centre movement.

The Continuing Development of Community Control

The basic idea behind notions of community or consumer control is that the actual or potential clients of a law centre should be setting the centre's policies and priorities for work. This is to be achieved through a management committee, the majority of whose members should be the 'consumers' of the law centre's services. In this way law centres are supposed to remain aware of and responsive to local needs and any changes therein.

From the outset of the law centre movement the operationalization of the concept of community control has been characterized by two features: diversity and difficulty. Indeed, there have been examples of fully – operating law centres that, for a time, had no management committee at all. It is not an easy concept to operationalize for it depends both on the willingness of local people to come forward for election to a management committee, and on their abilities to function within that structure and not to be intimidated by any professional members of the committee. Byles and Morris's (1977: 14 – 16) study highlighted a problem – typical during the formative years of the movement, but less so today – of management committees being dominated by lawyers and other professionals. Since then improvements have been made, and the Law Centres' Federation has organized training courses for those consumers and lay people who are involved in the management of law centres.

While distinct steps have been taken to ensure the concept becomes more of a reality, the diversity in forms of management committee has remained. Thus, the Leicester Rights Centre – a second tier agency – does not have a management committee composed of a majority of ordinary clients. Instead it is made up mostly of 'people who work in other advice agencies or who otherwise have some special knowledge or experience of the Centre's work' (Leicester Rights Centre, 1987 – 8:i).

More typical is the system whereby anyone living within the catchment area of a law centre may apply to become a member, and it is from this membership that the management committee is elected each year. Law centres vary as to whether there are standing sub – committees of the management committee with responsibilities for reporting back on specific issues. Equally, there is variation in the number and kind of individuals who may be co – opted to serve on a management committee. Furthermore, there is no empirical evidence of which I am aware to indicate whether those who do become members of law centres are representative and typical of the populations served by those respective centres. Moreover, there are neither extensive data on the extent to which individual management committees take a positive lead in policy formation, nor on the extent to which they may be essentially a 'rubber – stamp' – albeit with a power of veto – for initiatives generated by law centre staff, who are responsible for the day – to – day operation of centres. Indeed, at some law centres the staff are represented on the management committee, while at others they are specifically denied any direct representation.

What can be said, however, is that there appear to be differences between centres in their abilities to build up memberships. For example, Ealing Community Law Centre (1988:2) reported that one of its biggest difficulties was finding local people willing to commit time and energy to the centre as members of the management committee. Yet at Gloucester Law Centre (1987 – 8:12), where membership of the management committee is divided into sections with places reserved for disadvantaged people and community groups, the recruitment to the committee has been very successful with eleven women and ten black persons on the 1987 – 8 management committee.

While it is, therefore, fair to say in respect of management committees that law centres have actively been engaged in learning from the mistakes made in the early days of the movement, the lessons relating to high individual caseloads have proved to be more difficult, if not to learn then certainly to implement.

The Caseload Problem Revisited

I have already indicated that law centres have had to cope with growing demands for advice and representation throughout the 1980s. Adamsdown Community Law Centre (1985–7:10), for example, cited a 14% increase in net workload in 1985–6, and a further 17% increase in 1986–7. Such large growths in demand have frequently outstripped increases in funding. However, I am not so much interested in the increases themselves as in the manner in which the services are delivered, and in how the continuation of an open–door, reactive delivery mechanism perpetuates many of the problems described in Chapter Four when I was analysing the work of law centres in the 1970s.

There are numerous examples of law centres still struggling to overcome the problems of an overly reactive approach, despite at least a decade in which many of them might have learned the lessons of focusing too heavily on individual casework. Of course, one answer to this point is simply to refer to the overwhelming demand from individual clients with which law centres have to cope. What else can they do but treat individual unmet need as best they can? It is a decent sentiment but it is not the whole issue. Many centres actually want to *avoid* the worst excesses of an overly reactive delivery system but have still failed to do so. Although the service at Hyson Green Law Centre (1984–5:2), for instance,

> is firmly based on individual day–to–day casework, whenever possible we also work with groups of local residents, tenants' groups, ethnic groups, in seeking to tackle their problems in a collective way...Sadly, at least from the staff's point of view, the enormous demand for individual work has meant that this aspect has taken a secondary role.

Even a centre with a more strongly articulated proactive approach may not be immune to the problems of high individual caseloads. Avon and Bristol Law Centre (1984–5:6) is an agency that

> still sees working with groups as being a more effective use of...limited resources than working with individuals. However, the amount of individual casework has increased and, if allowed, could take up all of our time. As we are open to the public from 10am to 4pm each day, it is obviously difficult to forecast demand, and, despite a good referral system, a lot of staff time is spent on reception duties.

Law centres have often tried to alter their ways of working, such as UCLC in the late 1970s, in order to mitigate the worst effects of an individualized casework approach, but they have not always found a successful outcome. For instance, Brixton Community Law Centre (1984–5:2) reported that

> ...the major change was the implementation of a split between project and caseworkers. The idea was that a singleminded approach to projects would achieve greater

results. The reality was that the pressure on the caseworkers, who incidentally are expected to do all the advice work as well, was too great and the system was abandoned as the year closed. We have now returned to the system where each worker shares in advice, case and project work as before.

Too high a level of casework can have deleterious effects on both staff morale and on the quality of services available to clients[11]. The chairperson of Tower Hamlets Law Centre (1987 – 8:2), in a statement that would reflect the situation in many other law centres, has noted how often he has seen his law centre's staff working long hours into the evenings in order to cope with the volume of cases. Manchester Law Centre (1983 – 4:5) reported that:

It is a source of considerable concern to the staff that as the volume of work continues to grow, the quality of the service – certainly in terms of time available to deal with the individual's problem – has to be sacrificed.

Concern to provide as professional a service as possible is an obvious goal of law centres. Hounslow Law Centre is an interesting example of how efforts to improve quality were undermined by too high a caseload. The individual caseload at the centre had been

so heavy that the system of accepting clients has had to be changed. Attempting to deal with clients' problems when they first call at the Centre led to long waits for the clients and frustration for members of staff on reception who found it impossible to devote themselves adequately to a client's problem while dealing with telephone queries and answering the door – bell to receive new clients (Hounslow Law Centre, 1983 – 4:2).

The new system of making appointments for clients so that they could return to the centre and be seen by staff specializing in their problem areas meant that clients received 'a much better service, and staff are deriving satisfaction from being able to provide such a service' (Hounslow Law Centre, 1983 – 4:2). This is a perfectly proper way for a law centre to try to resolve the issue at hand, but it also happened to be a method that elevated legal casework to a pre – eminent position. It can be difficult to extricate oneself from such a position where nearly all efforts are channelled towards the greater efficiency and quality of the individualized casework approach, as Hounslow itself has found. Responding to a growing demand for welfare rights advice by increasing the number of workers dealing with such issues, the centre nevertheless found that it was 'hard pressed to meet the demand...to advise and represent in this field' (Hounslow Law Centre, 1983 – 4:37). More recently, in a further attempt to improve the quality of its services, Hounslow Law Centre conducted an internal review of its activities. Despite the adoption of another reception method a quarter of the centre's staff was engaged in reception duties, which it was felt was proving an obstacle to servicing existing casework. The centre raised the possibility that it might in the future adopt a closed – door policy, only taking clients on referral from other agencies, as a way of overcoming this obstacle (Hounslow Law Centre, 1987 – 8:1).

However, the adoption of a closed – door policy may not prove to be the answer, especially in areas where people have got used to the idea that their local law centre is a place they can simply 'pop into' for help. Indeed, even a centre originally set up as a closed – door agency has encountered difficulties in developing a more fully proactive approach as a counterbalancing influence to the reactive, individualized, style of delivery. Oldham Law Centre was created in May 1988 as a closed – door centre only taking referrals from advice agencies in priority areas. It is mainly a casework agency, which is building up its individual caseload and therefore has not yet encountered case overload. One of its constitutional requirements is to carry out educational work, not simply with individuals and groups, but also in terms of training courses and the preparation of a range of advice and information leaflets. This is the area where the agency has achieved the least so far, and due to a shortage of resources none of the planned leaflets has got beyond a draft stage. Indeed, the plan to produce them has been shelved indefinitely (Oldham Law Centre, 1988 – 9:8). A similar process has happened at the Southwark Law Project (1988:6) where in January 1989 each worker had an active caseload of over 100 files. 'High caseloads make it hard to respond to new demands quickly, or to make time for the information and education side of law centre work'.

Law centres have adopted a number of plans – albeit often unsuccessfully – to try to bring the caseload problem under control, but a few still open for business with what can only be described as either breathtaking optimism or extreme naivety. One visitor to Gateshead Law Centre argued that since the centre was relatively new, it had the advantage of being able to learn from the mistakes of other law centres (Law Centres' Federation, Winter 1985:5). The centre, however, appeared not to have learned these lessons.

> Although it was originally *hoped* that there would be an equal balance between case work, advice and education work, and group work, some 50% of the staff's time is presently taken up with individual case work, and the staff are putting some effort into redressing the balance (Law Centres' Federation, Winter 1985:5, Italics added).

A similar situation occurred at Gloucester Law Centre, which within months of opening had to cope with the problems of its own success. 'All of this success does mean that the staff already feel in danger of being overloaded with casework' (Law Centres' Federation, December 1985:11). This remark came from a law centre that hoped 'it has learnt from the errors made by existing Law Centres so that it does not, at the very least, repeat them' (Law Centres' Federation, December 1985:11). However, there are occasions when this can seem a forlorn hope, as the final example of Wolverhampton Law Centre (1987 – 8:10, Italics added) shows.

When the Centre was originally founded [in February 1985] it was accepted that much of the work of the staff would be client centred. However, *it was hoped* that the staff would also be involved in education and campaign work. In practice the staff has discovered that the demands of casework have been overwhelming. Thus they devote the vast majority of their time to their caseloads. Indeed such is the volume of cases that all staff members work long hours of overtime, much of it unpaid. The [Staff Working] Group is greatly concerned about this on two counts. Firstly, we have become alarmed at the sheer volume of casework that the centre has to cope with and the effects that this is having on the staff both physically and mentally. Secondly, we are concerned that the amount of casework makes it very difficult to pursue the education and campaign work that is part of the Centre's function.

Of course, it is not the fault of law centres that there are in so many neighbourhoods such vast pools of unmet legal needs. Indeed, with the growing dissatisfaction among some private solicitors concerning what are perceived to be low rates of remuneration for Legal Aid work, firms are withdrawing from the scheme with the consequent outcome that more clients are likely to want to use the services of law centres and other advice agencies (Newham Rights Centre, 1988 – 9:5). However, law centres can be criticized for apparently believing – despite overwhelming evidence to the contrary – that it is possible to create an open – door law centre and subsequently implement a successful policy that not only brings individual case numbers under control, but also leads to a *significant proportion* of proactive work being carried out. Given the extremely large demand for law centre services and the current levels of inadequate resources, there is only one way in which a centre could deliver a significant proportion of its services in a predominantly proactive manner; and that is to structure the law centre from the outset as a closed – door, group – orientated agency. For a variety of reasons the law centre movement may not favour such a policy on any large scale, and the issue of reactivity versus proactivity is one I shall return to in the final chapter. But whatever the views of the law centre movement it should at least recognize the naivety of much of its planning or lack of it hitherto. That is to say; a predominantly reactive law centre cannot be turned into a centre which is much more proactively orientated simply by tinkering around its operational edges. While individual casework and its servicing remain paramount in the perceptions and activities of law centre staff, the possibilities for a significantly proactive approach are likely to be undermined.

Notes

1. The Greater London Council (GLC) allocated funds to the Hillingdon Legal Resource Centre, a voluntary agency that had emerged after the closure of the original centre, whose funds had been cut off by the borough council. Also in 1981 the GLC funded the Wandsworth Legal Resource Project that emerged from the closure of the borough's three law centres in the previous year. Money from a variety of sources was also obtained to create the Brent Young People's Law Project. Thamesdown Law Centre in Swindon also opened in 1981.

2. For instance, in February 1985 the Department of the Environment refused further Urban Programme funds to Stockwell and Clapham, and North Lambeth law centres. Strathclyde Regional Council voted to reduce the 1985–6 budget of Castlemilk Law Centre by thirty percent.

3. While the Conservative Government appeared to be indifferent to law centres, they had been endorsed throughout 1985 by the Labour, Liberal, and SDP parties; by the TUC; and by the Church of England in its report *Faith in the Cities* (LCF, December 1985:1). Despite these endorsements hard financial decisions were being taken by other bodies to the detriment of some law centres, such as Paddington Law Centre, which faced possible closure after Westminster City Council in December 1985 voted to refuse further support. As an aside, the threat to Paddington and to several other law centres around this time was accompanied by the 'usual' response of the movement in the shape of details of the opening of a new centre – this one in Gloucester in September 1985.

4. The start of the year also brought the ironic news that just as Camden Law Centre was planning to move into new premises in March 1986, so in the same month Paddington Law Centre was scheduled for closure. Paddington did close but in June 1986 the London Borough Grants Committee, a body set up after the abolition of the GLC, decided to provide funds to reopen the centre.

5. Very similar quotations can be found (normally in the introduction or in the preface by the chairman or chairwoman of the management committee) in the annual reports of a number of law centres, for example; UCLC (1987–8), Brixton Community Law Centre (1987–8), and Plumstead Community Law Centre Ltd (1987–8). Ironically, in July 1989 I was informed by Newcastle Law Centre that the centre couldn't even afford to publish annual reports.

6. North Lambeth Law Centre (1988–9:1) was another that reported this combination of increased demand and reduced resources. In its case the reduction in resources came from a 7% cut in the local council's grant. The increased demand –

reflected in many other law centres too – came from changes in housing, social security, and immigration law.

7. Of course, if a centre suffers what West Hampstead Community Law Centre (1987 – 8:1) referred to as 'massive' cut in funding, then it is hardly surprising that the quality and quantity of a centre's services would be adversely affected.

8. Many centres, such as the Southwark Law Project (1988:11), are forced to maximize income from Legal Aid. 'This is time consuming and does involve meanstesting clients'.

9. Southwark Law Project (1988:1) stated that it was only able to survive the preceding year 'by making a massive effort to increase...income from Legal Aid'.
   Saltley Action Centre (1987 – 8:3) reported that in 1987 – 8 approximately 27% (£32,952) of its annual income came from Legal Aid, mostly via the Green Form scheme. Even so, it ended the year with a deficit, which caused the centre to argue that it would have to boost its income from Legal Aid still more if it were to remain financially viable.

10. Increasing demands for advice on welfare benefits and the Social Fund were experienced at Avon and Bristol Community Law Centre (1988:6); Tower Hamlets Law Centre (1987 – 8:13 – 14); and at Newham Rights Centre (1988 – 9:6), to cite only a few.

11. For example, at Sheffield Law Centre (1988:1) an increase in one area of casework – enquiries about British nationality – could only be handled by curtailing or suspending work in other areas with the obvious deterioration in service for those bringing problems to the centre in the suspended or curtailed areas. These rather drastic ways of restricting demand are the kinds that were practised in the 1970s and are still being implemented in some centres in the 1980s. Thus, Saltley Action Centre (1983 – 4:5) found itself unable to cope at one period with the volume of advice and casework and decided to suspend temporarily its open – door policy.

7 Law centres in the future: the policy debate

A major theme of this book has been concerned with the idea of access to legal services and the facility (or otherwise) with which low–income people can secure their legal rights in the welfare law field. Law centres have played an important and innovative role in improving access and in pursuing their clients' claims. Another theme has focused on the level of the client's active involvement and participation in the actual pursuit of a solution to his claim. This is the theme of active citizenship[1], and I shall now consider what contributions law centres have made to its realization.   Much of this consideration revolves around the issues of individual casework and groupwork.

Operational Styles And Citizenship

According to Downie and Hatton, the casework – or lawyerist – approach in law centres is inherently limited. What is required to overcome its limitations is a greater proactive emphasis on community work. Community work's involvement with local groups encourages group members to participate directly in solving common problems and, thus, facilitates the development of individual competence and confidence. Downie and Hatton criticize the casework approach for individualizing the problems of clients and thereby preventing them from seeing the wider context of their grievances. Moreover, the ideas of professional expertise bound up in the lawyerist or casework approach hinder the development of the skills and competences of clients (Downie and Hatton, 1984:11). The problem, as they see it, is that there is increasingly less of an effective counterbalance to the lawyerist approach as community work activities are jettisoned or curtailed in many law centres. The reason for the decline of community work they attribute to the lack of a clear definition as to what constitutes community work so that it becomes an undertaking vulnerable to cutbacks in funding.

Other commentators are less concerned about the alleged need to have an influential counterbalance both to the philosophy of the casework approach and to its limitations, but are anxious that law centres should use their existing casework in an efficient manner. For instance, Smith (1986:6) has argued that the private profession, and not law centres, has dominated the welfare law market in financial terms. Not only have law centres received a small percentage (two percent) of all monies spent on public legal services (New Law Journal, 1983:1050), but also whereas 74% of Green Form expenditure is devoted to criminal and matrimonial work, which is largely conducted by private solicitors, only 5% and 2% respectively are spent on housing and welfare benefits work, the typical activity of law centres (Smith, 1986:6). Although law centres have tried a number of tactics to reverse their poor funding position relative to private practitioners conducting welfare law work, Smith has questioned whether this was the correct strategy. In his view law centres have actually generated work for the private profession and increasingly they appear to be

'super Citizens Advice Bureaux' whose major legal activity is diagnosis and referral. They have a high turnover of staff with both lawyers and non–lawyers averaging less than three years. They live in harmony with the advice–giving establishment and with most of the local authorities that fund them; although any opposition they encounter arises largely from their local campaigning role (Smith, 1986:6).

In contrast to this position, Smith has argued that law centres should grow into a national network, should 'take over' certain policy fields in the welfare law area, and should develop their work in respect of tribunal representation and emergency services. Attached to the national network would be a number of specialist resource centres to provide expert knowledge and to develop national policies in the field of welfare law. In this way, according to Smith, law centres would be able to explore the legal and social policy implications of their existing individual casework in a more efficient and productive manner.

Such a move would allow law centres to enjoy their casework and to celebrate it in a stream of pamphlets, policy documents, action and analysis, instead of almost apologising for it. It might encourage them to a more activist and open approach to legal services so that they submitted, for example, bids to run emergency services, or to set up innovative national projects (Smith, 1986:7).

It is not clear in Smith's article whether the stream of pamphlets and other activities would emerge from the specialist resource centres or from individual members of the network of law centres. As a way of reducing staff turnover and of creating a more challenging professional role for lawyers, Smith's suggestions have merit. However, it may be that the advantages would only apply to those working in the resource centres, while staff in the 'ordinary' law centres might still be so overcome by the demands of individual casework that they could not respond adequately to any policy issues engendered by those cases. Furthermore, Smith's scheme is highly legalistic. No doubt there would be some complex cases of great interest to lawyers that could set legal precedents or may contain important social policy implications, but the vast majority of cases, as now, will be routine. The problem remains, therefore, of how to respond to the mass of routine cases. To rely too much on the legalistic approach, where the lawyer dominates the professional – client relationship and where the client is normally in a passive role, is to overlook the possibility of introducing a greater emphasis on self – help and on client participation.

The different views of Downie and Hatton and of Smith reflect the differing emphases given to what is considered to be the proper role of law centres. If one sees law centres as specialist resource agencies lobbying on behalf of the welfare poor, the content of individual lawyer – client relationships becomes less important. If these agencies succeed as a pressure group the tangible benefits of their work will flow to the needy; some limited social change in favour of the poor will take place; and the issue of whether clients have developed legal and political competence becomes less compelling. There will be no need to engage clients actively in processing their own cases in order to enjoy the benefits stemming from successful completion; lawyers will provide the benefits on behalf of the poor. However, if one sees the role of law centres as helping poor people to understand the nature of their grievances and to participate in attempts to overcome them, the content of the lawyer – client relationship and the active involvement of the client are crucial issues. Each view of the proper role of law centres contains quite different implications for citizenship.

Such views often focus on the casework – groupwork balance. Brent Law Centre has attempted to combine both views by suggesting that there is no worthwhile distinction between casework and groupwork; it is the continuities that are important. Brent Law Centre has argued, first, that both types of work generate tangible benefits for identifiable individuals. Second, when law centre resources are scarce, controls on the level of casework are necessary not only to ensure the conduct of groupwork, but also to ensure the quality of casework itself. Third, both styles can be pursued 'strategically' so that legal resources are used to gain the best possible results for the community (Brent Community Law Centre, 1983:4). I have no argument with the first point, since it is axiomatic that when benefits accrue they do so in respect of individuals or individual group members. Brent's second proposition is also self – evident, but it fails to address the issue properly. While Brent acknowledges that its own closed – door is a mechanism for rationing scarce resources, it fails to explain how open – door law centres are to achieve control over the demands of individual casework in order to continue with their groupwork activities. Instead, Brent simply mentions some developments, such as the establishment of specialized units, that have already largely failed to achieve such a goal.

Brent Law Centre has argued that a law centre does not have to be a closed – door agency in order to do groupwork effectively. However, only a limited amount of groupwork is currently being carried on within law centres. This is hardly surprising given the levels of staff turnover and the chronic underfunding of many centres. Moreover, proactive undertakings, of which groupwork is a part, are difficult and, as we have seen in the experiences of many open – door law centres, the demands of individual casework have all too easily undermined proactive intentions and activities. When a law centre has a closed – door, such as Brent, or when it has a small catchment area so that individual casework levels are not too high, such as Adamsdown, there are possibilities to pursue more proactive policies. But the major issue is how can open – door law centres with 'normal' catchment areas and large demands for casework find ways of limiting this demand and developing the expertise to operationalize proactive aims. The experience of most law centres does not appear to have supplied the answer to this question.

Brent's third point – that casework and groupwork can be pursued strategically – similarly fails to address the whole issue. Of course, some individual cases have a strategic importance and some law centres conduct work with such a goal in mind. But most open – door, reactive law centres are struggling to cope with the flow of largely routine cases. Moreover, coping with this demand undermines their abilities to conduct strategic work whether it be individual or group orientated.

According to Brent Community Law Centre (1983:5), 'case work and group work are valuable and should not be seen as wholly divorced from one another as methods of providing legal services'. This is fine as far as it goes, and at Brent itself no doubt a constructive balance between the two has been forged. Indeed, Brent has pioneered much work of which the law centre movement may be justifiably proud, but we should not underestimate the role of the closed – door as a means of striking a balance and of pursuing such work. Open – door law centres have not, in general, been able to introduce as great an emphasis on proactivity as many of them would have liked. We should no longer delude ourselves that significantly more proactive goals will be implemented within law centres until the problem of excessive individual casework has been solved.

The Royal Commission and Law Centres

The debate within the law centre movement is not simply about philosophical differences concerning the structure of law centre services and operations, it also has important implications for the nature of citizenship. The Royal Commission on Legal Services (RCLS) had an opportunity to forge a more participatory role for clients in the work of law centres. Despite the fact that it recommended the creation of new citizens' law centres, it envisaged not active participating clients but passive individuals who could expect no more, in the main, than highly individualized and legalistic case processing of their claims. Had they ever been implemented, citizens' law centres would have offered a predominantly reactive (and means – tested) service to clients, with group and community work activities discouraged (RCLS, 1979:83 – 4) This kind of law centre would have referred even larger numbers of individual clients to the private profession than is the case today. As a clearing house or filter for the financial interests of the private profession, citizens' law centres would have left intact professional domination of the lawyer – client relationship and provided few opportunities for people to engage actively in addressing the nature of their own citizenship[2].

Naturally, law centres and the Law Centres' Federation (LCF) voiced many criticisms of the proposals made by the RCLS. In particular, the LCF pointed out that the Commission had misunderstood the role of community work in the operation of law centres, which allowed people to pursue self – help options and to learn more about their rights (LCF, 1980:15). The defence of community and groupwork activities was a clear feature of the LCF's *A Response to the Royal Commission on Legal Services* (1980). However, whereas the LCF's *Towards Equal Justice* (1974) was more strongly committed to the proactive approach, and its *Evidence to the Royal Commission on Legal Services* (LCF, 1977:38) spoke of the need 'to actively engage in promoting the creation of new organs of community expression', the examples cited in *A Response to the Royal Commission on Legal Services* do not emphasize the direct formation and organization of community groups. Rather, the emphasis is on working with existing groups.

A major theme running through the twenty nine examples of law centre activities contained within *A Response to the Royal Commission on Legal Services* (1980:16 – 20) is the idea of law centres acting as 'a resource for advice and information about the law and the procedures' (LCF, 1980:19). Indeed, many of these activities are described as nothing more than 'the provision of advice and assistance on matters relating to English law, albeit delivered in innovative fashion' (LCF, 1980:20). The Federation maintained that such a service was, or should be, uncontentious since the provision of such advice and assistance was perfectly legitimate. There is still scope within such an approach for developing informed consent, client competence, and participation. However, the former emphases on *creating* local groups and on pursuing legal and *non – legal* strategies appear no longer to be given priority. Indeed, the LCF's *The Case for Law Centres* (April 1989) makes no mention at all about group formation and non–legal activities, and in this sense the law centre movement has distanced itself somewhat from a wholehearted commitment to a more fully proactive style of operation. The emphasis now is largely upon opening up access to legal services, on providing self–help opportunities for clients, and on supplying information to community groups (LCF, April 1989:6).

In part, the 'retreat' from a more vigorous and fully developed proactive approach may be due to so many law centres experiencing difficulties in trying to operationalize it. In part, it may also be due to the realization among the movement that even a rhetorical commitment to the radical proactive alternative is likely to deter potential funding agencies.

The approach, or combination of approaches, adopted within law centres to the delivery of legal (and non–legal) services has an important influence on the manner in which citizenship rights are realized. An agency with an approach in keeping with the image of a 'super Citizens Advice Bureau', or in keeping with the RCLS's version of a citizens' law centre would diagnose client problems, provide some kind of advice, and refer a large number of individuals to private practitioners. There is little scope here for enhancing informed consent, client competence, or client participation. Those law centres that take on the role of specialist resource centres may lobby effectively on behalf of the poor who may well reap the benefits of law centre strategies. Few of these people, however, will have been actively involved in the process through which the benefits were gained. Once again, there is little here to enhance the notion of active citizenship status. It is in the few closed–door centres that the potential remains for a more participatory style in which clients are actively involved in seeking solutions to their problems and in which they play an integral part in those decision–making processes of direct relevance to them as citizens.

The Law Centre Movement, Politics And Finance

The way in which the law centre movement will develop depends on a number of important factors. The level and nature of client demand for legal services will obviously be crucial in influencing law centre operations, especially since law centres are subject, to varying extent, to forms of local community control. But that demand will also be modified by the structure of other advice–giving services existing alongside law centres. Also influential will be the developmental and lobbying work of the Law Centres' Federation; but, arguably, the most important element will be the financial and political climate facing the movement as a whole.

As we enter the decade of the 1990s that climate is still a severe one, which is seriously limiting the development of the movement.

For example, the Legal Aid Board, while agreeing to fund for 1990 – 1 the seven law centres previously financed by the Lord Chancellor's Department, has made no commitment beyond that date. The 7% increase in the grant to these law centres will not relieve the chronic underfunding of previous years (Legal Action Group, February 1990:5). The Central London Community Law Centre (1987 – 8:4), in a statement that would produce sad echoes in other law centres, reported that each year it faced a fresh financial threat to its survival, and that the creation of the Legal Aid Board was beginning to influence the funding of law centres by local authorities and charities because of the uncertainty about the Board's policies. At Brent Community and Young People's Law Centre a spirited defence was made of the cost – effectiveness of law centre services in respect of the local authority, such as the work of the centre in maximizing housing benefits for clients and thus helping to reduce rent arrears owed to the council. However, this did not save the centre from 'massive cuts of around 20%' (Brent Community and Young People's Law Centre, 1989:1).

Law centres require long – term and independent funding if they are ever to escape the financial uncertainties and crippling workloads currently oppressing their employees. Indeed, much of the heavy and increasing workload is the product of government policies and legislation that have created enormous demands for legal and welfare advice. Yet the actual financial position of law centres could not be further removed from the ideal expressed above.

> ...of the 60 law centres in the country it is fair to say that the majority are in financial crisis. Many are close to losing all their funding as a result of government cuts in grant or through cuts in local authority grants. The local authorities themselves see these cuts as an inevitable consequence of government controls on their spending...
> All around the concept of free legal advice is constantly under attack (North Lewisham Law Centre, 1988:2).

The position of North Lewisham and other law centres in such financial predicaments makes a mockery of the idea that law centres should be independent from their funding agents, whether these be central or local government[3]. The mechanism through which law centres receive their grants is such that they are virtually dependent on the goodwill of local authorities to continue to fund them, albeit at levels much below what is required to remove law centres from their chronically underfunded position. There is, perhaps, a certain futility in being independent of the funding agent, in the sense of a law centre being free to pursue its own areas of work without interference, if the level of funding is barely adequate to provide a proper service in the first place.

Of course, the principle of political independence is still of paramount importance as the experience of Bradford Law Centre highlights.

> Politicians found it difficult to understand why a Law Centre exists and why they fund a Law Centre that

expends some part of its energies challenging the Council. The Left have wanted to 'municipalise' us – to absorb us into the general services it offers the public; the Right to cut us adrift from Council funding. Both approaches perhaps betray a similar misunderstanding about the role and the function of a Law Centre (Bradford Law Centre, 1988:2).

That role is to provide advice and assistance for the legally indigent; to satisfy unmet legal needs; and to alert citizens to their legal rights.

In this way law centres are helping to fill the service gaps inherent within the system of Legal Aid and within the private profession as whole. Indeed, one of the original reasons for the creation of law centres was to overcome the deficiencies of private practice. Moreover, there will inevitably be occasions when in seeking to represent the rights of clients law centres will come into conflict with local authorities, many of which provide the major funding for the centres. It says very little for politicians' respect for the democratic freedoms of citizens that they should be so wary of being challenged in the courts and elsewhere about their policies. As Bradford Law Centre (1988:5) correctly points out, no local authority should fund a law centre and expect to place restrictions on the rights of individuals to pursue justice, even if this pursuit does involve a client who has a legitimate grievance against the local council. This does not mean that the law centre should not be accountable to the local authority for the manner in which it spends public funds. It does mean, however, that law centres should be free from political interference in the cases they represent.

There is a more subtle way, however, in which the work of law centres is denigrated by government; in this case by central government. Access to justice is both a value – concept and a mechanism. We speak highly of British justice and have set in place all manner of mechanisms whereby citizens can avail themselves of the judicial process. Law centres are a relatively new mechanism in this area. Whatever their funding problems, internal operational difficulties, and lingering doubts about what has been claimed for 'consumer control', law centres have been successful. As Gifford (1986:90) put it: 'Law centres have proved their worth throughout the legal world'. But it would seem they have yet to prove their worth to central government. The government has been urged on many occasions to provide adequate funding for law centres on the basis that they are cost – effective agencies supplying a high quality service to the public. Gifford (1986:93) has argued:

Whether people have access to legal help is such a fundamental issue that it should not depend on the chance of living within the boundaries of a local authority which is prepared to fund a law centre. The basic funding of law centres should be taken out of the present insecurity and confusion and become the responsibility of the Minister of Justice.

However, because of the failure of the government to adopt a policy of secure funding for law centres (and to create a Ministry of Justice), access to justice is still fragmented and many poor people, in particular, are denied their legal rights. The government response is to say that the creation and funding of law centres are primarily local issues, which is to overlook the serious financial difficulties facing many councils as a direct result of government policy.

Thus it is that access to Marshall's concept of justice or to Galanter's notion of legality are still governed by chance and inequality. Poor people are still a long way from being guaranteed the right to pursue their grievances on equal terms with others, to hold officials accountable, or to participate in decision – making forums. The development of a national network of law centres, adequately funded, can only be achieved with the strongest possible commitment of central government to the goal of comprehensive access to justice for citizens. It is to be regretted that in this country, which places so much value on the idea of justice, we do not have the financial and policy initiatives to ensure the development of a network of law centres. Even though currently central government is not interested in such a framework of initiatives, that does not mean that a financial and operational structure for the future role of law centres should not be considered.

Law Centres In The 1990s And Beyond

The current position of law centres is unsatisfactory in two major ways. First, the existing network of centres, both in terms of the resources of individual agencies and of its geographical coverage as a whole, is unable to satisfy the levels of client demand. Second, law centres are unable to offer sufficient career development and occupational challenges for the professionals they employ. Too many lawyers are doing nothing more than routine legal advice work, laced with some representation, while others – such as community workers – are impeded in pursuing their main educational and outreach functions because of a combination of insufficient resources and the onerous demands of individual casework. If law centres are to overcome these current deficiencies a more secure financial future and a more effective operational structure will have to be implemented. My own ideas for such a structure – often drawing on those of the Law Centres' Federation – are set out below. They cannot be realized unless central government is prepared to make the necessary political and financial commitment to such a scheme.

Funding

As long ago as February 1984 the Law Centres' Federation prepared *Design Brief for a National Funding Policy for Law Centres.* It argued for central funding of law centres provided by an appropriate government department or intermediary body. The funding should consist of three elements. Core funding would provide for centres of adequate size to meet client demands and to be able to employ a minimum of four full – time staff, including at least two lawyers, in each centre. This kind of funding should be made available on a stable and continuing basis, subject to review periods of a minimum of four years and also subject to the supply of annual reports and audited accounts. Supplementary funding should be made available, as deemed appropriate in various law centres, to provide additional specific posts or projects. Centres would be able to bid against a fixed pool of central finance for such posts so that innovative projects allegedly of value to the community could be developed. If proven to be valuable the costs of the project or post would be subsequently subsumed under a centre's core funding. Finally, there should be support funding to underpin research, the development of new centres, the training of staff and management committee members, and various other back – up services. Primarily, the Law Centres' Federation would receive the resources to ensure the development of support and back – up services (LCF, February 1984).

The above proposed method of funding has much to commend it, for the following reasons. First and most importantly, it envisages secure long – term funding for law centres. This will allow centres and local communities *to plan* more effectively how they should respond to local and changing needs. It will also help to recruit more people with high professional standards who are currently understandably anxious about the continued existence of some centres. It would release law centres from the almost annual round of expending precious resources on trying to obtain renewed funding and would do much to increase morale within the movement as a whole. Second, the LCF's proposals recognize the need for *extra* resources, via supplementary funding, to pursue non – casework activities. That is not to say that these extra posts would never be involved in individual casework projects, only to highlight the fact that projects of a more proactive kind require careful planning and sufficient resources. The competitive bidding system for supplementary funding should meet both criteria in that only carefully planned bids ought to be acceptable and, if accepted, they should then be assured of decent funding. Third, the funding for support services recognizes both the valuable work of the Law Centres' Federation itself and the need to expand its role in disseminating good practice and in supplying expert advice on new technology, management, accounting, and training.

In order to justify to government the worth of these funding proposals and to demonstrate the cost – effectiveness of law centres, the Federation decided to create a '*framework of evaluation* designed to provide criteria that accurately reflect the performance of law centres' (LCF, 1984 – 6:7, Original italics). With a grant from the Nuffield Foundation in 1985 the Federation produced *Questions of Value* (1988), which was a statement of the principles upon which the evaluation of law centre work should take place, as well as an attempt to encourage good evaluative practice. The evaluation exercise and the data generated have been useful to the movement and have possibly helped law centres to defend themselves against those who say that law centres must prove their worth. As yet, however, central government has not been convinced of the need to fund a national network of law centres, despite the many arguments presented to it in favour of such a development.

Local Control and Flexibility

It is important that, wherever possible, law centres be demand – led; that there should be a local need for their services; and that the potential consumers of those services be involved in setting up and in running the law centres. Here steering groups and, subsequently, management committees have a vital role to play. It is not the function of a management committee to control the day – to – day operation of a law centre, but to set policies and priorities for action so that the centre is constantly responding sensitively and effectively to local needs and demands. In this way law centres can remain accountable to their consumers and clients.

The Law Centres' Federation has played an important role in helping to train those who are members of management committees and it has argued that the majority of the membership should be drawn from the local community and not be composed of representatives of professional bodies or local councils. However, as the Federation itself admits, the principle of local community control operates in varying forms throughout the movement (LCF, April 1989:6). The LCF's evaluation study has gone some way towards addressing the issue of community control, but what needs to be developed in the context of some future national network of law centres, is a common structure of management by consumers. Granted that management committees allow for local flexibility but this does not mean that logically there ought to be large variations in the structure, composition, functions, and powers of such committees. On the contrary, the receipt of large amounts of public funds to any future network of law centres will require that the issue of accountability is thoroughly debated and a common format agreed upon.

The principles on which to base such a format should include the following. The majority of the people sitting on a management committee should be members of the law centre. Membership should be open to individual consumers or potential consumers living within the centre's catchment area who come forward and request membership. The members would elect management committee representatives from among their number by a secret postal ballot. The centre's staff should also be entitled to one or at most two representatives on the committee, to be elected by the staff as a whole. The Law Centres' Federation should also have one representative, selected by the Federation from among the ranks of

146

what would be an increased staff complement under any scheme to create a network of law centres. This representative would be able to advise on new developments taking place in other centres and to offer management expertise, if requested. At the discretion of the full management committee a small number of co – opted members may be invited to sit on the committee. This number should not be so large as to undermine the majority position enjoyed by the consumers of the law centre's services.

There is no need to have representatives in any form from funding agencies, unless they be observers; nor is there a need to have representatives from the national or local law societies and other professional associations. These latter individuals are unlikely to have any expertise that is not already contained within the management committee and their absence would make it less likely that the proceedings of the committee would be dominated by the few remaining professionals. The accountability of the law centre for the use of public funds can be better fulfilled through the publication of annual reports and audited accounts than through representatives of funding bodies sitting on the management committee. It may also be fulfilled through a proper evaluative study that may be made from time to time on each law centre, conducted in partnership by representatives from the Law Centres' Federation and research personnel from the central funding agency. The findings of such studies could be used, in part, not only to determine the suitability of law centres to receive further public funds – as assessed on the fulfilment of agreed performance indicators – but also to disseminate good practice throughout the movement.

In this way law centre staff and management committees would be aware of national standards in the quality of service, which they would have to reach, but would remain free to fashion the work of their respective agencies to meet the particular needs of differing localities.

Careers and Remuneration

Law centres are experiencing difficulties in recruiting and retaining suitably qualified staff. The advent of long – term core funding for law centres would help to overcome some of these difficulties. Indeed, the availability of supplementary funding – given to law centres on a three year basis, if required – opens up the possibility of lawyers and other professionals joining law centres for a limited period to work on specific projects. These projects may be related directly to the occupational interests of those filling such posts, or they may be in the form of paid secondment from one's normal employment. As such, private practitioners, and social and community workers may wish to undertake certain projects within law centres, especially if the secondments are at an early stage in their careers and they are seeking to gain greater experience.

An adequately funded and national network of law centres would also be able to offer much better professional training in a number of areas, but particularly for those seeking 'articles', or whatever other forms of legal certification are implemented. Such a development would also introduce the work of law centres to a much wider professional audience, especially if law centres were commonly to contract with law schools and other professional training bodies to provide supervised placements and other learning opportunities.

Salaries, however, for professional staff – especially lawyers – would have to bear some comparison with those in the private sector. Salaries would be a major element in the funding of a network of law centres, but not so large as one might first think. Many lawyers in any future network of law centres will be those starting out on a law career who will enter the salaried sector in the first instance because of the challenge and wide experience to be gained from working within a law centre. After three to six years many of these will move on to other kinds of legal work outside law centres. Although there will still, therefore, be a turnover of staff, this need not lead to general upheaval and to a loss of expertise. Law centres will, in a future network, be training many more of the lawyers they will require, and these people will very quickly build up their knowledge of and expertise in the poverty law fields. Indeed, law centres will, to some extent, be able to generate their own replacements for those who leave to pursue their careers elsewhere. Since many will stay only a relatively few years they will not be too expensive to employ.

Money, however, will have to be available to retain those lawyers who would prefer to stay within law centres for considerably longer periods of time. These highly experienced lawyers will require a suitably generous pay scale, as indeed will other kinds of employees who are pursuing a long-term commitment to law centres. Many current law centre workers may argue that this undue emphasis on legal personnel and on the argument to provide generous pay scales for them will undermine the focus in some centres on parity of pay between staff. My response to that concern is to argue that despite the laudable goals behind pay parity, the occupational market place rarely operates according to such egalitarian sentiments. Thus, law centres may simply have to be prepared to remunerate lawyers at scales close to the market rates if they are to retain highly qualified and experienced staff.

However, there is another factor, beyond levels of pay, that influences the attitude of law centre workers to their jobs; namely, job satisfaction. This is a subject that I shall cover in the next section devoted to the structure and distribution of law centre services for all these topics are intricately entwined.

A National Law Centre Network

In 1984 the Law Centres' Federation argued that by 1989 there should be at least one hundred law centres in the UK (LCF, February 1984:4). In 1990 there are only sixty, and even tr estimate of one hundred was probably understated since little account was taken then of the need for law centres in rural areas[4]. It is almost impossible to say exactly how many law centres there should be, especially if one adheres to the view that the creation of new centres should be predominantly demand or consumer – led. And in any event how many there 'should' be is likely to be closely related to the sum of money that may be made available to set up the network. What concerns me here is not the total number of law centres that may come into existence, but the manner in which their services should be organized.

In my scheme law centres would be arranged regionally, with the boundaries of each region and the number of its constituent law centres being revised from time to time as new law centres are created as part of the network. Within each region, which would include rural as well as urban areas, law centres would have to fulfil two functions. First, they would have to meet individual client demands for advice and assistance in matters of poverty and social welfare law, and also to supply similar advice to other welfare and advice agencies that request it. Second, they would have to undertake proactive work in the form of project work, educational activities, groupwork, and so on. Because of the huge demand from poor and low – income individuals for what is mostly routine advice and assistance, I envisage this kind of work being conducted by several open – door law centres within each region. If necessary, this service should also have a mobile dimension so that law centre staff are able to hold advice sessions in what would otherwise be inaccessible areas of the region. Given that these law centres would be better resourced, have more effective training schemes for employees, and have more support services, the work of open – door agencies should not be as onerous and, at times, unsatisfying for staff as has been the case until now.

Moreover, staff in the open – door centres would also be eligible to rotate for a period of time to a closed – door centre pursuing proactive work, at least one of which would also be set up in each region. This rotation would mean staff could transfer expertise and experience gained in the open – door centre to a closed – door environment; an environment in which there would be existing knowledge about how to implement effectively ideas for proactive undertakings. Proactive work would not, therefore, be carried out in isolation by individual members of staff, but rather would be developed as the work of a *proactive agency* whose rationale was solely based on this kind of operational style. Proactive centres would pursue legal and non – legal strategies and, in addition to working with existing groups in each region, they would be empowered to create new community – based organizations. These centres would seek to implement high levels of informed consent, client competence, party upgrading, and citizen participation. The staff rotation system would also provide opportunities to pursue what may be seen as different or more challenging work to that in the open – door law centres. At the very least, it would provide a break from servicing the needs of individuals. On leaving a closed – door centre, staff would be returning to open – door centres with expertise that might be valuable in helping to improve the quality of their own service. In this way, job satisfaction ought to be significantly improved.

Both kinds of law centre would have management committees. Open – door law centres would have representatives elected from among their respective memberships. In turn, closed – door centres would have management committees composed of representatives elected from the committees of the open – door centres in the region. The proactive work that a closed – door centre and its staff wished to pursue would, therefore, have to be discussed and ratified by that centre's management committee, which would be composed of a majority of consumers of law centre services drawn from throughout the whole region.

Moreover, since the closed – door centres would also be able to pursue non – legal strategies of action in combination with legal tactics, there would be a better prospect of overcoming what Scheingold (1974) has referred to as the 'myth of rights'. The myth of rights is founded on the mistaken believe that winning one's case in a court of law automatically leads to the enjoyment of tangible benefits. In fact, as with many cases of housing disrepair, a tenant may gain a declaration of his right to live in habitable property only to find long delays on the part of the landlord before any repair work is undertaken. To Scheingold legal rights are important mobilizing forces, since people are prepared to fight politically for what they believe they are entitled to. Awareness of legal rights is therefore a valuable attribute of the competent citizen, but the pursuit of those rights need not be confined simply to legal strategies.

These intra – regional and operational divisions between open and closed – door centres would, I believe, allow the movement to capitalize on all that is best in the two approaches while lessening some of the difficulties associated in the past and present with the reactive style. In particular, the bureaucratic and participatory emphases (Chapter One) would be combined to good effect within each region so that open – door law centres would provide a comprehensive and equitable service to individuals seeking help, which is one of the advantageous aspects of the bureaucratic approach. At the same time, the realization of community control in open – door centres should lessen the less favourable bureaucratic tendencies towards professional domination of the agency, lack of accountability, and inflexibility in responding to client needs. Closed – door law centres would pursue a more participatory ethos in which the knowledge and expertise of non – professionals are especially valued, and where the major goal is to involve citizens wherever possible in those decision – making processes that impinge on their lives.

Of course, in order to make a practical reality of these proposals a great deal more detailed work would have to be undertaken. My concern, based on the assumption of adequate long – term funding, was to outline the broad structure and principles on which a national network of law centres could be developed so that it would satisfy a number of crucial needs. Among these is the need to supply a high quality service appropriate to the demands of clients. But also of vital importance is the necessity to construct an effective and genuine form of community control, and to provide a rewarding and challenging career for law centre employees. Finally, any such network must incorporate a significantly proactive focus in addition to the individual casework it pursues. I believe that my outline proposals for a network of law centres are capable of satisfying the needs I have mentioned. But why include the proactive focus as one of the elements in the activities of a national network of law centres? The answer to that question is to be found in a final consideration of the worth of citizen involvement in the pursuit of the rights of citizenship.

Law Centres, Participation, And Democracy

The central issue here is to explore how law centres in a modern, complex, and democratic state can safeguard and expand the rights of citizens.

Competence and Proactivity

As Friedmann (1971) has noted, whereas the means of administration by the state have grown larger, more bureaucratized, specialized, and often highly technical, the means of representation have lagged behind. Despite the expansion of the state's role as a kind of umpire, in terms of the various powers invested in Legal Aid, tribunals, and social welfare legislation, many citizens and especially the disadvantaged have found it increasingly difficult to participate in the proliferation of state policies and functions. Nonet (1971:58) has argued that increasingly it has been the perceptions of officials that have moulded the rights and responsibilities of citizens as opposed to these rights and duties being defined directly by those most affected.

Only a competent citizenry can forge a more participatory relationship that links the rule – makers with those who must abide by the rules. A competent citizen takes advantage of opportunities to exercise the rights of citizenship; but first opportunities must be created and citizens must be equipped with the necessary skills to benefit from them. It is here that the proactive, closed – door law centre can play an important role. As I have indicated in earlier chapters, it is the proactive law centre that seeks to realize high levels of informed consent, to operationalize people – working techniques, and to upgrade the capacity of its clientele to take collective legal and non – legal action. Thus do proactive law centres endeavour to increase the skills, confidence, and competence of clients. Moreover, they encourage clients to become involved in decision – making forums beyond those of the court and the tribunal.

Of course, there are difficulties in seeking to achieve these goals. Proactive work is difficult; it requires a form of professionalism in which experts are prepared to share their knowledge with lay people; there have been funding problems with proactive centres because of political opposition to this kind of delivery mechanism; there are the uncertainties involved in group formation and the need to avoid groups becoming dependent on law centre expertise. However, none of these problems is insuperable, especially in the context of a network of law centres with proactive agencies operating at the heart of each region.

Another caveat concerns the extent of political power that small community groups can expect to wield and, therefore, the extent of social change in favour of the poor that can be achieved. Granted a tenants' association, for example, will never command the resources of the local housing department or of the Department of the Environment. But that is precisely why we have a system of law so that, in theory, rights and wrongs can be adjudicated irrespective of differentials in wealth, resources, and power. The fact that the legal system, in practice, is to some extent influenced by these differentials is another reason why proactive law centres pursue non – legal as well as legal strategies. Both strategies are legitimate ways in which citizens are trying to assert their rights, and the possibility that the extent of social change brought about as a result of that exercise may be limited should not inhibit people from pursuing what they believe they are entitled to. The participation of a competent citizenry in a wide range of decision – making forums would be a valuable democratic development in its own right. Moreover, there are other benefits to be gained.

Professional and Lay Expertise

One of the most important benefits that lay people can bring to decision – making processes is their own knowledge; their own expertise. This requires, however, that professionals are prepared to listen to them. Dennis's study of slum clearance schemes in Sunderland highlighted what happens when the professionals don't listen. Dennis demonstrated that the demographic information gathered by the expert planners and the statistical analyses they performed were not cautious and realistic approaches to slum clearance, but over – confident predictions based on uncertain assumptions (Dennis, 1970:108). Planning decisions about slum clearance had been approached as if they were simply technical forecasts, when in fact they involved complex issues about the housing preferences of a large number of households with different needs. There was very little consultation between residents and planners about these preferences.

The interests of the consumer, individually and collectively, played, then, a minor part in the formulation of the 1965 – 70 slum – clearance proposals. To some extent his interests were considered relevant to the decision, but no attempt was made to ascertain what those interests were: the decision was reached by using an incorrect and outdated stereotype of the slum family, eager and impatient to be granted improved accommodation. To a large extent, however, the consumer's self – perceived interests were regarded as a miscalculation, pernicious to himself and as a datum worthless to the official (Dennis, 1970:345).

Unable to participate in decisions about their own homes, the majority of residents who objected to demolition and rejected the alternative accommodation were ignored. The result, argued Room (1979:120), 'was a violation of residents' civil, political and social rights'. Indeed, such action on the part of expert planners questioned their very legitimacy. Dennis's answer to this question was to argue for the desirability of lay participation in decision – making processes on the basis that residents are knowledgeable about their own housing conditions in ways that outside experts can never be. Moreover, while the expert planner may be technically competent, he knows little about the social values of those who will be affected by the plans. He can only find out what those values are by consultation. In short, the planner requires a good deal of 'information from the only "experts" available, the people themselves' (Dennis, 1970:353).

The lessons from Dennis's work may be applied in other areas, and not limited to the topic of slum clearance. His study showed that the policy and decision – making process is incomplete without the insights that a competent citizenry can bring to it. As Room has noted, when communities respond to policy – making proposals by exploring courses of action that are appropriate to their own needs and values, they are essentially 'engaged in a critique of the wider society, although such critique and action are inchoate without...professional servicing' (Room, 1979:244).

Proactive law centres can provide such servicing as they combine lay and professional expertise as a means of seeking the participation of citizens in the policy and decision – making process. This does not mean that professional interests are eclipsed by those of lay people; but it does connote a greater participatory role for citizens. Without such participation policies may turn out to be ill – focused, poorly designed, or inappropriate.

Citizenship and Democracy

The work of law centres, both reactive and proactive, is not simply about the localized grievances of clients; it is also concerned with the relationship of the client to the state, and the extent to which the citizen is dependent upon the state or is able to make his own decisions in participation with state interests. When reactive law centres make clients more aware of their legal rights, they are less

153

likely to be dependent and passive recipients of state services. When proactive centres create participatory opportunities for clients, they too are likely to become more articulate in voicing their own claims. A competent citizenry is essential to the constructive functioning of what Marshall has called the 'democratic – welfare – capitalist' society.

At the macro level the nature of the democratic and capitalistic elements of society is decided respectively via the ballot and the market place, in which the actions of individuals lead directly to democratic and economic outcomes (Marshall, 1981a:107). Within the economic and democratic elements there remain, of course, many conflicts and inequalities, as is the case with the welfare element in Marshall's schema. However, whereas individuals have more of a direct impact on the nature of the first two elements, the provision of welfare in British society cannot be described in the same way. On the whole, welfare provision is the product of decisions taken by political leaders and various professionals, and citizens are often the passive recipients of what it has been decided they require.

The attainment of full citizenship would not spell the end of all inequalities. Rather the interplay between the political, social, and civil elements of citizenship and the manner in which they are expressed institutionally is one of the bases on which social integration is maintained within our society. Even so, inherent in the concept of citizenship are principles of equality. When these are set against existing social and economic inequalities they provide a means by which we can not only understand social conflict, but also can better plan for social amelioration. Nowhere is this more important than in the regulation of the distributive benefits stemming from welfare provision. Given that welfare provision ought to be related to the satisfaction of actual needs, it is imperative that the state, the professions, *and* the citizenry play an active role in policy – formulation in order to identify these needs more accurately, and more effectively allow for their satisfaction.

Marshall's civil right to justice and Galanter's access to legality are means by which individuals and groups may seek to realize the rights of citizenship. In asserting their claims citizens are giving substance to the interplay between the three elements of citizenship and are helping to give concrete form to the manner in which various institutions distribute benefits. This is part of the process by which the ebb and flow of social struggle and debate concerning the nature and content of policy – making is conducted. It is also a part of the continuing development of the nature of citizenship and of our understanding of its related rights and benefits.

Reactive, open – door law centres can play a part in helping individuals to realize some of their rights of citizenship. But we must go beyond simply providing access to legal advice; we must also develop proactive agencies, which can equip people with the necessary competences to *participate in decision – making forums*, for this is the ultimate goal of active citizenship. Community control of law centres is an important matter, but communal control over events that affect the citizenry is even more so, especially when one realizes how much valuable information citizens can contribute to the policy – making process. It is the fulfilment of the proactive and participatory approaches that holds out the greatest promise that citizens will have a greater measure of control over their own lives. In conclusion, law centres, and particularly proactive agencies, can make a contribution not only to the legal process, but also to the democratic bases of society.

Notes

1. The term active citizenship should not be confused with the concept expounded in the late 1980s and in 1990 by the Conservative Party, which is partly about the desirability of individuals giving money to charity, and about teaching children the duties of the 'good citizen', and so on. It is used in this book in a specialized away and is a development of Marshall's (1976) ideas on citizenship.

2. For a fuller critique of the RCLS's recommendations in respect of law centres see Stephens (1982).

3. Guidelines for law centres, setting out the principle of independence from funding agents and the control of law centres by local management committees were suggested in 1978 by the Labour Government Lord Chancellor, Lord Elwyn – Jones. They were later endorsed by the Conservative Government Lord Chancellor, Lord Hailsham (Brighton Law Centre, 1986:4).

4. For a recent study of the position of legal advice services in a rural area see Kempson (1989).

Bibliography

Annual reports of law centres are to be found at the end of the main bibliography.

ADAMSDOWN COMMUNITY AND ADVICE CENTRE,(Summer 1976), *Disrepaired Roads and Pavements. A Report and do it yourself Kit on enforcing section 44 of the Highways Act 1959.*
ADAMSDOWN COMMUNITY TRUST,(1978), *Community Need and Law Centre Practice. An Empirical Assessment.*
BATTEN,T.R.,(1975), *The Non–Directive Approach in Group and Community Work*, Oxford University Press, London.
BELLOW,G.,(1977), 'Can Legal Services Help the Poor?', *Working Papers for a New Society*, Spring, pp.52–60.
BENNETT, Jr.,W.S. and HOKENSTAD, Jr.,M.C.,(1973), 'Full–time People Workers and Conceptions of the "Professional"', in P.Halmos (ed), Professionalisation and Social Change, *The Sociological Review Monograph*, No.20, Keele University, pp.21–45.
BLACK,D.J.,(1973), 'The Mobilization of Law', *Journal of Legal Studies*, Vol. 2, pp.125–49.
BRENT COMMUNITY AND YOUNG PEOPLE'S LAW CENTRE,(1989), *Coming of Age in the Inner City.*
BRENT COMMUNITY LAW CENTRE,(1983), *Legal Services in the Inner City.*
BUCHER,R., and STRAUSS,A.,(1960–1), 'Professions in Process', *American Journal of Sociology*, Vol.66, pp.325–34.
BYLES,A., and MORRIS,P.,(1977), *Unmet Need: The Case of the Neighbourhood Law Centre*, Routledge and Kegan Paul, London.

156

CAMPBELL,C.,(1976), 'Lawyers and their Public', *The Juridical Review*, Part 1, April, pp.20 – 39.

CARLIN,J.E.,(1962), *Lawyers on their Own*, Rutgers University Press, New Brunswick.

CARLIN,J., and HOWARD,J.,(1965), 'Legal Representation and Class Justice', *University of California Los Angeles Law Review*, Vol.12, pp.381 – 437.

CHAKRABORTY,T., ROBINSON,C., and DABEZIES,C.,(1988), *Coming of Age: North Kensington Law Centre 1970 – 1988*, North Kensington Law Centre, London.

DENNIS,N.,(1970), *People and Planning*, Faber and Faber, London.

DEPARTMENT OF THE ENVIRONMENT,(October 1983), *Streamlining the Cities: Government Proposals for Reorganising Local Government in Greater London and the Metropolitan Counties*, Cmnd. 9063, HMSO, London.

DOWNIE,S., and HATTON,K.,(1984), 'Working in Communities', *Law Centres' News*, Summer, No.19, pp.10 – 11.

FOSTER,K.,(1973), 'The Location of Solicitors', *Modern Law Review*, Vol.36, pp.153 – 66.

FRIEDMANN,W.,(1971), *The State and the Rule of Law in a Mixed Economy*, Stevens and Sons, London.

GALANTER,M.,(1974), 'Why the "Haves" come out ahead: Speculations on the Limits of Legal Change', *Law and Society Review*, Vol.9, No.1, Fall, pp.95 – 160.

GALANTER,M.,(1976), 'Delivering Legality: Some Proposals for the Direction of Research', *Law and Society Review*, Vol.11, No.2, Special Issue, pp.225 – 46.

GIFFORD,T.,(1986), *Where's the Justice? A Manifesto for Law Reform*, Penguin Special, Harmondsworth.

HADLEY,R., and HATCH,S.,(1981), *Social Welfare and the Failure of the State*, George Allen and Unwin, London.

HALSEY,A.H.,(1984), 'T.H.Marshall: Past and Present', *Sociology*, Vol.18, No.1, February, pp.1 – 18.

HAMMERSMITH and FULHAM LAW CENTRE,(September 1989), *Law Centre Bulletin*.

JOHNSON,T.J.,(1972), *Professions and Power*, Macmillan, London.

KATZ,J.,(1976), *Routine and Reform: A Study of Personal and Collective Careers in Legal Aid*, Northwestern University, Sociology Department, PhD thesis.

KEMPSON, E.,(1989), *Legal Advice and Assistance*, Policy Studies Institute, London.

KRAMER,R., and SPECHT,H.,(eds),(1975), *Readings in Community Organization Practice*, second edition, Prentice – Hall, Englewood Cliffs, New Jersey.

LADINSKY,J.,(1963), 'Careers of Lawyers, Law Practice and Legal Institutions', *American Sociological Review*, Vol.28, pp.47 – 54.

LAW CENTRES' FEDERATION,(1974),[originally called Community Law Centres], *Towards Equal Justice, Memorandum of Evidence by the Law Centres' Working Group to the Lord Chancellor and his Advisory Committee*.

LAW CENTRES' FEDERATION,(1977), [formerly, the Law Centres' Working Group], *Evidence to the Royal Commission on Legal Services*.

LAW CENTRES' FEDERATION,(1980), *A Response to the Royal Commission on Legal Services*.

LAW CENTRES' FEDERATION,(Summer 1980), *Law Centres' News*, No.6.

LAW CENTRES' FEDERATION,(Spring 1982), *Law Centres' News*, No.11.

LAW CENTRES' FEDERATION,(Autumn 1982), *Law Centres' News*, No.13.

LAW CENTRES' FEDERATION,(Winter 1982 – 3), *Law Centres' News*, No.14.

LAW CENTRES' FEDERATION,(November 1983), *The Case for Law Centres*.

LAW CENTRES' FEDERATION,(1984), *Response to the White Paper 'Streamlining the Cities'*.

LAW CENTRES' FEDERATION,(1984 – 6), *Annual Report 1984 – 5, and 1985 – 6*.

LAW CENTRES' FEDERATION,(February 1984), *Design Brief for a National Funding Policy for Law Centres*.

LAW CENTRES' FEDERATION,(Winter 1985), *Law Centres' News*, No.21.

LAW CENTRES' FEDERATION,(October 1985), *The Case for Law Centres*, 2nd edition.

LAW CENTRES' FEDERATION,(December 1985), *Law Centres' News*, No.24.

LAW CENTRES' FEDERATION,(1988), *Questions of Value: A Framework for the Evaluation of Law Centres*.

LAW CENTRES' FEDERATION,(April 1989), *The Case for Law Centres*, 3rd edition.

LAW CENTRES' WORKING GROUP: see LAW CENTRES' FEDERATION, (1977).

LAW SOCIETY,(1968), *Legal Advice and Assistance*.

LAW SOCIETY,(1969), *Legal Advice and Assistance*.

LAW SOCIETY,(August 1989), *Franchising Legal Aid*.

LEGAL ACTION GROUP,(February 1990), *Legal Action*.

LEGAL AID ANNUAL REPORTS: see LORD CHANCELLOR'S OFFICE.

LORD CHANCELLOR'S OFFICE,(1967), *17th Legal Aid Annual Reports*, HMSO, London.

LORD CHANCELLOR'S OFFICE,(1979 – 80), *30th Legal Aid Annual Reports*, HMSO, London.

LORD CHANCELLOR'S OFFICE,(1980 – 1), *31st Legal Aid Annual Reports*, HMSO, London.

LORD CHANCELLOR'S OFFICE,(1982 – 3), *33rd Legal Aid Annual Reports*, HMSO, London.

LORD CHANCELLOR'S OFFICE,(November 1983), *The Government Response to the Report of the Royal Commission on Legal Services*, Cmnd.9077, HMSO, London.

LORD CHANCELLOR'S OFFICE,(1983 – 4), *34th Legal Aid Annual Reports*, HMSO, London.

LORD CHANCELLOR'S OFFICE,(1984 – 85), *35th Legal Aid Annual Reports*, HMSO, London.

MARSHALL,T.H.,(1976), 'Citizenship and Social Class', in T.H.Marshall, *Class, Citizenship and Social Development*, Greenwood Press, Westport, pp.65 – 122.

MARSHALL,T.H.,(1981a), 'Value Problems of Welfare Capitalism', in T.H.Marshall, *The Right to Welfare and Other Essays*, Heinemann, London, pp.104 – 22.

MARSHALL,T.H.,(1981b), 'Reflections on Power' in T.H.Marshall, *The Right to Welfare and Other Essays*, Heinemann, London, pp.137 – 53.

MAYHEW,L.H.,(1975), 'Institutions of Representation: Civil Justice and the Public', *Law and Society Review*, Vol.9, No.3, Spring, pp.401 – 29.

MORRIS,P.,(1973), 'A Sociological Approach to Research in Legal Services', in P.Morris, R.White, and P.Lewis, *Social Needs and Legal Action*, Martin Robertson, London.

NEW LAW JOURNAL,(1983), 'The Case for Law Centres', Vol.133, Friday 2nd December, pp.1049 – 50.

NONET,P.,(1969), *Administrative Justice: Advocacy and Change in a Government Agency*, Russell Sage Foundation, New York.

NONET,P.,(1971), 'Legal Action and Civic Competence', in J.Floud, P.Lewis, and R.Stuart (eds), *Proceedings of a Seminar: Problems and Prospects of Socio – Legal Research*, Organized under the auspices of the Nuffield Foundation at Nuffield College, Oxford, June – July, pp.50 – 9.

NORTH KENSINGTON NEIGHBOURHOOD LAW CENTRE,(1980), *The First Ten Years*.

PARKER,J.,(1979), *Social Policy and Citizenship*, Macmillan, London.

PARLIAMENTARY DEBATES,(May 1985), House of Lords, *Official Report*, Vol.463, 8 May, HMSO, London.

PARLIAMENTARY DEBATES,(July 1985), House of Commons, *Official Report*, Standing Committee D, Administration of Justice Bill [Lords], 6th sitting, Thursday 4 July (morning and afternoon), HMSO, London.

PARLIAMENTARY DEBATES,(17 February 1986), House of Lords, *Weekly Hansard*, No.1315, 17 – 20 February, HMSO, London.

PARLIAMENTARY DEBATES,(13 March 1986), House of Commons, *Weekly Hansard*, No.1375, 10 – 14 March, HMSO. London.

PINKER,R.,(1979), *Social Theory and Social Policy*, Heinemann, London.

PODMORE,D.,(1980), *Solicitors and the Wider Community*, Heinemann, London.

POLLOCK,S.,(1975) *Legal Aid – The First 25 Years*, Oyez, London.

PRIOR,R.B.L.,(1984), *Law Centres: A Movement at a Halt*, Conservative Political Centre.

REPORT OF THE ADVISORY COMMITTEE ON THE BETTER PROVISION OF LEGAL ADVICE AND ASSISTANCE,(1970), Cmnd.4249, HMSO, London.

ROOM,G.,(1979), *The Sociology of Welfare*, Basil Blackwell and Martin Robertson, Oxford.

ROSENTHAL,D.,(1976a), 'Evaluating the Competence of Lawyers', in L.Brickman and R.Lempert (eds), *The Role of Research in the Delivery of Legal Services: Working Papers and Conference Proceedings*, The Resource Center for Consumers of Legal Services, Washington,D.C., May, pp.109 – 42.

ROSENTHAL,D.,(1976b), 'Evaluating the Competence of Lawyers', *Law and Society Review*, Vol.11, No.2, Special Issue, pp.257 – 85.

ROTHMAN,J.,(1968), 'Three Models of Community Organization Practice', in *Social Work Practice 1968*, Selected Papers of the 95th Annual Forum National Conference on Social Welfare, San Francisco, 26 – 31 May, pp.16 – 47.

ROYAL COMMISSION ON LEGAL SERVICES,(1979), *Final Report*, Cmnd 7648, HMSO, London.

RUESCHEMEYER,D.,(1964), 'Doctors and Lawyers: A Comment on the Theory of the Professions', *Canadian Review of Sociology and Anthropology*, Vol.1, pp.17 – 30.

SCHEINGOLD,S.,(1974), *The Politics of Rights*, Yale University Press, New Haven and London.

SHEFFIELD CITY POLYTECHNIC SOCIOLEGAL STUDIES GROUP,(1978), *The Effectiveness of Sheffield Free Legal Information Service: An Empirical Study*, Dept of Economics and Business Studies, Sheffield City Polytechnic.

SMITH,R.,(1986), 'Law Centres: Where to Now?', *Legal Action*, June, pp.6 – 7.

SOCIETY OF CONSERVATIVE LAWYERS,(1968), *Rough Justice*, Conservative Political Centre.

SOCIETY OF LABOUR LAWYERS,(1968), *Justice for All*, Fabian Research Series, No.273.

SPERGEL,I.A.,(1975), 'The Role of the Community Worker', in R.M.Kramer and H.Specht (eds), *Readings in Community Organization Practice*, 2nd edition, Prentice – Hall, Englewood Cliffs, New Jersey.

STEPHENS,M.R.,(1982), 'Law Centres and Citizenship: The Way Forward', in P.Thomas (ed), *Law in the Balance: Legal Services in the Eighties*, Martin Robertson, Oxford.

WHITE,R.,(1975), 'The Distasteful Character of Litigation for Poor Persons', *The Juridical Review*, Part 3, December, pp.233 – 51.

ZANDER,M.,(1966), 'Poverty and the Law', *Socialist Commentary*, September, pp.13 – 5.

ZANDER,M.,(1978), *Legal Services for the Community*, Temple Smith, London.

Unpublished Manuscript Sources

URBAN COMMUNITY LAW CENTRE,(1973), *Constitution.* [hereafter UCLC].
UCLC,(March 1976), *Parity of Pay Scales.*
UCLC,(1976), *Report of the Meeting of Law Centre Workers,* 7 November 1976.
UCLC,(June 1977), Internally distributed mimeographed paper [untitled] prepared by UCLC lawyer for discussion at the staff meeting held on 16 June 1977.
UCLC,(1978a), *Work of the Centre,* Paper prepared by one the centre's lawyers and by a general worker.
UCLC,(1978b), *Draft Five Year Report,1973 – 78.*
UCLC,(June 1978), Internally distributed mimeographed paper [untitled] prepared by a UCLC general worker.

Published Law Centre Annual Reports

(Other published materials by law centres are found in the main bibliography)

ADAMSDOWN COMMUNITY AND ADVICE CENTRE,(1975), *Annual Report to Members 1974/75.*
ADAMSDOWN COMMUNITY LAW CENTRE,(1985 – 7), *Two Year Annual Report 1985 – 6, 1986 – 7.*
ANNUAL REPORT OF HACKNEY ADVICE BUREAU AND LAW CENTRE,(1976 – 7), *Law Centre Report.*
ANNUAL REPORT OF HACKNEY ADVICE BUREAU AND LAW CENTRE,(1977 – 8).
AVON and BRISTOL COMMUNITY LAW CENTRE,(1988), *Annual Report.*
AVON and BRISTOL LAW CENTRE,(1984 – 5), *Annual Report.*
BALHAM NEIGHBOURHOOD LAW CENTRE,(1973 – 4), *(1st) Annual Report.*
BALHAM NEIGHBOURHOOD LAW CENTRE,(1974 – 5), *Annual Report.*
BALHAM NEIGHBOURHOOD LAW CENTRE,(1975 – 6), *Annual Report.*
BALHAM NEIGHBOURHOOD LAW CENTRE,(1976 – 7), *Annual Report.*
BALHAM NEIGHBOURHOOD LAW CENTRE,(1977 – 8), *Annual Report.*
BRADFORD LAW CENTRE,(1984), *Annual Report.*
BRADFORD LAW CENTRE,(1988), *Annual Report.*
BRENT COMMUNITY LAW CENTRE,(1975), *First Report.*
BRENT COMMUNITY LAW CENTRE,(1976), *Report.*
BRENT COMMUNITY LAW CENTRE,(1979), *Report.*
BRIGHTON LAW CENTRE,(1986), *Review and Annual Report.*
BRIGHTON LAW CENTRE,(1988), *Annual Report.*
BRIXTON COMMUNITY LAW CENTRE,(1984 – 5), *Annual Report.*

BRIXTON COMMUNITY LAW CENTRE,(1987 – 8), *Annual Report.*
CASTLEMILK LAW CENTRE,(1988 – 9), *Annual Report.*
CENTRAL LONDON COMMUNITY LAW CENTRE LTD,(1987 – 8), *Annual Report and Accounts.*
CENTRAL LONDON LAW CENTRE,(1984), *Annual Report.*
DUDLEY LAW CENTRE,(1987 – 8), *Annual Report.*
EALING COMMUNITY LAW CENTRE,(1988), *Annual Report.*
GATESHEAD LAW CENTRE,(1988 – 9), *Annual Report.*
GLOUCESTER LAW CENTRE,(1987 – 8), *Annual Report.*
GREENWICH COMMUNITY LAW CENTRE,(1988), *Annual Report.*
HAMMERSMITH and FULHAM COMMUNITY LAW CENTRE,(1987), *Annual Report.*
HANDSWORTH LAW CENTRE,(1978 – 9), *Annual Report.*
HIGHFIELDS and BELGRAVE LAW CENTRE,(1984 – 5), *Annual Report.*
HILLINGDON LEGAL RESOURCE CENTRE,(1986 – 7), *Annual Report.*
HOUNSLOW LAW CENTRE,(1983 – 4), *Annual Report.*
HOUNSLOW LAW CENTRE,(1987 – 8), *Annual Report.*
HYSON GREEN LAW CENTRE,(1984 – 5), *The First Four Years. Incorporating Annual Report 1984/85.*
HYSON GREEN LAW CENTRE,(1987 – 8), *Annual Report.*
ISLINGTON COMMUNITY LAW CENTRE,(1975), *Annual Report.*
LAMBETH COMMUNITY LAW CENTRE,(1975 – 6), *Annual Report.*
LAMBETH COMMUNITY LAW CENTRE,(1977 – 8), *Annual Report.*
LEICESTER RIGHTS CENTRE,(1987 – 8), *Annual Report.*
LIVERPOOL 8 LAW CENTRE,(1987 – 8), *Annual Report.*
MANCHESTER LAW CENTRE,(1983 – 4), *Annual Report.*
MIDDLESBROUGH LAW CENTRE,(1988), *Annual Report.*
NEWHAM RIGHTS CENTRE,(1974 – 5), *Report and Analysis of a Community Law Centre.*
NEWHAM RIGHTS CENTRE,(1977), *Two Years Work, 1975 – 77.*
NEWHAM RIGHTS CENTRE,(1988 – 9), *Annual Report.*
NORTH KENSINGTON LAW CENTRE,(1987), *Annual Report.*
NORTH KENSINGTON NEIGHBOURHOOD LAW CENTRE, [hereafter N.Kensington NLC] (1971), *Report.*
N.KENSINGTON NLC,(1972), *Report.*
N.KENSINGTON NLC,(1973), *Report.*
N.KENSINGTON NLC.(1974), *Report.*
N.KENSINGTON NLC,(1975), *Annual Report.*
NORTH LAMBETH LAW CENTRE,(1988 – 9), *Annual Report.*
NORTH LEWISHAM LAW CENTRE,(1984), *Annual Report.*
NORTH LEWISHAM LAW CENTRE,(1988), *Annual Report: Tenth Anniversary.*
NORTH MANCHESTER LAW CENTRE,(1987), *Annual Report.*
NORTHERN NEIGHBOURHOOD LAW CENTRE,(1974), *1st Annual Report.*

NORTHERN NEIGHBOURHOOD LAW CENTRE,(1974-5), *Report*.
NORTHERN NEIGHBOURHOOD LAW CENTRE,(1975-7), *Report*.
OLDHAM LAW CENTRE,(1988-9), *Annual Report*.
PADDINGTON ADVICE AND LAW CENTRE,(1976-8), *Annual Report*.
PADDINGTON LAW CENTRE,(1986-7), *Annual Report*.
PADDINGTON NEIGHBOURHOOD ADVICE BUREAU AND LAW CENTRE,(1975), *Annual Report*.
PADDINGTON NEIGHBOURHOOD ADVICE BUREAU AND LAW CENTRE,(1976), *Annual Report*.
PLUMSTEAD COMMUNITY LAW CENTRE LTD,(1987-8), *Annual Report*.
ROEHAMPTON and PUTNEY COMMUNITY LAW CENTRE,(1987-8), *Annual Report*.
SALFORD LAW CENTRE,(1988-9), *Annual Report*.
SALTLEY ACTION CENTRE,(1983-4), *Annual Report*.
SALTLEY ACTION CENTRE,(1987-8), *Annual Report*.
SHEFFIELD LAW CENTRE,(1988), *Annual Report*.
SMALL HEATH COMMUNITY LAW CENTRE,(1976-7), *First Annual Report*.
SMALL HEATH COMMUNITY LAW CENTRE,(1977-8), *2nd Annual Report*.
SMALL HEATH COMMUNITY LAW CENTRE,(1978-9), *3rd Annual Report*.
SOUTHALL COMMUNITY LAW CENTRE,(1984-5), *Annual Report*.
SOUTHALL COMMUNITY LAW CENTRE,(1987-8), *Annual Report*.
SOUTH ISLINGTON LAW CENTRE,(1987-8), *Annual Report*.
SOUTH MANCHESTER LAW CENTRE,(1988), *Annual Report*.
SOUTHWARK LAW PROJECT,(1988), *Annual Report*.
SPRINGFIELD HOSPITAL,(1986-8), *Advice and Legal Representation Project at Springfield Hospital. Biennial Report*.
STOCKTON ON TEES LAW CENTRE,(1988), *Annual Report*.
STOCKWELL and CLAPHAM LAW CENTRE,(1988), *Annual Report*.
THAMESDOWN LAW CENTRE,(1988-9), *Annual Report*.
TOTTENHAM NEIGHBOURHOOD LAW CENTRE,(1986-7), *Annual Report*.
TOWER HAMLETS LAW CENTRE,(1987-8), *Progress Report*.
URBAN COMMUNITY LAW CENTRE,(1974), *Annual Report*.
URBAN COMMUNITY LAW CENTRE,(1974-5), *Annual Report*.
URBAN COMMUNITY LAW CENTRE,(1975-6), *Annual Report*.
URBAN COMMUNITY LAW CENTRE,(1977-8), *Annual Report and 5 Year Review*.
URBAN COMMUNITY LAW CENTRE,(1984), *10 Year Review*.
URBAN COMMUNITY LAW CENTRE,(1984-6), *Annual Report*.
URBAN COMMUNITY LAW CENTRE,(1986-7), *Annual Report*.

URBAN COMMUNITY LAW CENTRE,(1987 – 8), *Annual Report.*
VAUXHALL COMMUNITY LAW CENTRE,(1974 – 5), *Second Annual Report.*
VAUXHALL COMMUNITY LAW CENTRE,(1976 – 7), *Fourth Annual Report.*
WARRINGTON COMMUNITY LAW CENTRE,(1987 – 8), *Annual Report.*
WEST HAMPSTEAD COMMUNITY LAW CENTRE,(1987 – 8), *Annual Report.*
WOLVERHAMPTON LAW CENTRE,(1985 – 6), *Annual Report.*
WOLVERHAMPTON LAW CENTRE,(1987 – 8), *Annual Report.*
WOLVERHAMPTON LAW CENTRE,(1988 – 9), *Annual Report: Re – Launching for the 1990s.*

Index